Evelyn

A Novella
by

Susanna Sheehy

2014 Susanna C. Sheehy

This novel is a work of fiction. Any references to historical events; to real people, living or dead, or to real locales are intended only to give the fiction a sense of reality and authenticity. Names, characters, places, and incidents either are the product of the author's imagination or are used fictitiously, and their resemblance, if any, to real live counterparts is entirely coincidental.

All rights reserved. This book is printed in the United States of America. No part of this book may be used or reproduced in any manner whatsoever without written permission except in the case of brief quotations embodied in critical articles and reviews. For information address inquiries to:

Elden Publishing, LLC
susannasheehy@susannasheehy.com

Book cover design by Elden Publishing, LLC
Editing by Emily Sheehy Henderson

ISBN: 978-0-9789271-3-4
Library of Congress Control Number: 2015906702

Copyright information available upon request

**Other books
by
Susanna Sheehy**

The Second Half Trilogy

Marking Time
Book One

Second Half
Book Two

Crossed Lines
Book Three

Local Talent

Plastic Diamonds

Grand Passion

Novels are available at Amazon.com, BarnesAndNoble.com. They are available for order at local book stores and are also available in the Kindle and Nook stores.

Visit Susanna at:
www.susannasheehy.com and follow her on Facebook.

Chapter 1

Evelyn pulled into the driveway of her family home and stopped to take a long look. It had been only a little over five years since she'd gone away to school. She had finished her undergrad and masters in record time, and had come home for all the holidays and some weekends. The university was only about an hour away. Still it felt good to be coming home to stay. Not that she intended to live here with her parents for long. She had plans.

The long driveway wound down a gradual hill to an iron gate that led into a walled acre. The house sat on top of a small rise.

She opened the car door and got out. She wanted to savor the moment. She was coming home. She planned to get her own apartment soon, but for now she would just enjoy being home. The view was spectacular of rolling hills, two barns, black fencing. It was like a picture. She'd often wished she could paint it, but she couldn't paint.

Evelyn stepped onto the plush grass at the side of the road. It felt lovely under her feet. Her father was and had always been a devoted landscape artist. All twelve acres of the place showed it.

Wham! Something hit her in the back knocking her onto her belly. As she landed with her head turned to the right, she saw the back tire of her car as it rolled past her. Oh man, she'd forgotten to put on the parking break. She jumped to her feet and ran after the moving vehicle. The open door slammed shut with the momentum.

Realizing she couldn't catch the car she started to scream, hoping to warn any animals that might get in the way. The car bounced across the ditch on the side of the driveway and crashed through the fence, losing momentum as it rolled up the slight incline toward the barn. It came to a stop after it crawled up the side of the barn and landed at an angle on the outside wall.

Her father peered around the open door of the barn at the car. Then he looked up at her. He grinned widely, and waved as if nothing out of the ordinary had happened.

2 / Evelyn

She started to laugh, a bit hysterical, and as the tears began to flow she hurried down the driveway.

Jeff Landrum put down the bucket of feed he was holding and hurried toward his daughter. "There's my girl!" He picked her up and swung her around.

"Woah, Dad," she said. "You almost made me bump heads with Doris." She put her hand out to steady herself on the horse that had followed her father out of the barn.

"Look what I did. I could have killed someone." She buried her face in the horse's neck and shuddered.

"Well, you didn't. Look around. We're all just fine. Even the chicken's got out of the way. We're all pretty resilient. Remember we've known you all your life." He laughed. It was a warm comforting sound. He pulled her away from the horse and held her against his chest. It felt so good. He was a big man, six feet four inches in his youth. At 70 something years old he wasn't as tall, but he was still big and very strong.

"Why am I so clumsy?" Evelyn was giggling again. "And why do I have this stupid nervous laugh?"

"I don't know what worries me the most, the laughing or the crying." He held her away from him to look her up and down. "Oh honey, no one is hurt except you. Your cheek is skinned. The palms of your hands are skinned, and your jeans are torn at the knees. Let's go get you cleaned up." Putting his arm across her shoulders he guided her in the direction of the gate.

"What about the car?" She turned to look at the new convertible her parents had given her for graduation. "What about the fence?"

"I'll put Doris and Elmo in their stalls until I patch the fence. I think I can back the car off the barn wall." He laughed. "If not, we'll call a tow truck. It doesn't look like it's damaged. Don't worry about it."

Evelyn looked over at Elmo. The mule stood in the corner of the pasture munching grass. He probably hadn't even noticed the commotion.

"Is everyone alright?" Amanda Landrum ran toward them from the house. "I watched it all happen from the upstairs landing." Evelyn fell into her mother's arms as a fresh wave of tears and giggles erupted. Her mother was small, but not as small as Evelyn and her twin sister Alice. She pressed Evelyn's head to her shoulder and rocked back and forth.

"Ev, honey, you have to remember to put your car in gear and turn it off when you get out. It would have held even without the emergency break if it had been in gear." She looked up at Jeff. "I told you I didn't think a standard transmission was a good idea."

"She likes driving a stick shift." Jeff put his hands on both of their backs and pointed them toward the house. "She'll get the hang of it."

"I can't believe I'm so stupid."

"You graduated Magna Cum Laude. You're not stupid, clumsy maybe, but not stupid." He laughed and kissed her on the forehead. "Now you take her to the house, Amanda, and clean up her wounds. I'll put Doris and Elmo away and patch the fence. I'll be up in a few minutes."

When Jeff came into the kitchen a few minutes later Amanda was kneeling in front of Evelyn bathing her knees. Evelyn had changed into a pair of shorts and was looking at her scraped hands.

"This looks very familiar." He laughed.

"Yeah," Evelyn sighed. "I've always been the clumsy one."

"Alice has skinned up her knees a few times over the years." Amanda stood a little stiffly and stretched her back.

Evelyn watched. Her parents were getting old. She and Alice had been born late. She tried to remember their ages. Her dad was somewhere in his early seventies and her mother, late sixties.

"How old is Doris now?" She asked. Maybe focusing on the horse would get rid of the lump in her throat.

"She's thirty-two. Why?"

"I noticed she walked with a limp. Why? Is she injured or something?"

"No. She just has arthritis." Jeff washed his hands at the sink. "Just like your old man. We both limp on the same side. Isn't that kind of cute?"

"How is the knee, Dad?"

"It's doing very well. I was worried when they did the replacement. But I'm actually hiking again."

"That's great. You'd hate to give that up. Well," Evelyn stood up. "I'm going to take a shower before dinner. I'll be down in a while." She ran up the back stairway to her bedroom and closed the door.

She sat down on the bed and looked around the room. It hadn't changed since she'd left it five years ago. She walked to the window and looked out. There was a goldfish pond in the front yard. Her window looked out over it. There was a light in it that illuminated the water. You could see the fish swimming. There was a small fountain that did little more than bubble. It was a peaceful spot. It was a memorable spot for her. She looked at the stone bench beside the pond. She'd been kissed for the first time there. She'd never forget it, and she'd never forget the boy who'd kissed her.

She put her hand to her belly as it quivered at the thought. What was he doing now? She hadn't forgotten him, even though he had been unreachable for the last three years. They'd continued to see each other after she'd gone to school. He had come to the university a few times to see her. She had come home as many weekends as she could. Then something had changed.

Jamie had never talked to her about it, even though she'd asked. He just said he thought they should stop seeing each other. He said it was over. Maybe it was over for him, but it was definitely not over for her.

She knew he wasn't married or anything. Her sister would surely have known, and she would definitely have told her. What was the problem? Now that she had finished school she intended to find out and she intended to change it. She wasn't giving him up.

*

"So, where is Alice's new apartment?" She asked at dinner. "I never did even see the last one. She sure moves around a lot."

"She's never been able to sit still." Amanda laughed. "She was born that way."

"It's not far from the nursery. You know the complex across the pond." Jeff sat back and sipped the glass of tea in front of him. "That was a delicious meal, Manda," he said to his wife.

"Yeah, Mom, thanks for fixing my favorite. I love your barbecue chicken sandwiches."

"I'm glad you liked it."

"Aren't those apartments really old, Dad? I think they've been there since I can remember."

"They sure are old. They were built when your great-grandfather first sold off that part of his land. Back when he started growing landscaping plants instead of corn and cotton, back when he opened. They aren't bad, though. I'm sure they've been renovated several times."

"I'm sure Alice has put her personal mark on her apartment."

"She always does." Amanda stood up to clear the dishes.

"Yeah, then she moves to another apartment and puts her mark on that one." Evelyn laughed and stood to help her mother clear the table. "Relax, Mom. Let me do the dishes tonight. When I'm finished, I'm going to call Alice and go over there if she's home."

"Aren't you tired after your trip?" Jeff stood and put his hand on her shoulders.

"Dad, Athens is only an hour and a half from here. I'm not tired. Anyway, I won't stay late. I can't wait to start work in the family business, and no!" She raised her hand as her father started to object. "I am not going to take some time off before I start work. I've been preparing for this my whole life."

*

"You cut your hair!" Evelyn stood in the doorway of her sister's apartment. "It's just like mine. How will people tell us apart?"

"I thought it might be fun to be identical again. I don't think we've worn our hair the same since the second grade." Evelyn felt like she was looking in a mirror. They both had the same shade of brunette hair and the same pale shade of blue eyes. Without the different hairstyle, most people couldn't tell them apart.

"You wanted to be an individual, remember, not just a replica of your sister. I believe those were your words."

"Well, I want to be a twin now. I've missed you, Ev." Her sister threw her arms around her, dragged her bodily into the apartment and shut the door.

"Alice." Evelyn gently separated herself from her sister's bear hug, which was surprisingly like her father's bear hug. "We've seen each other frequently over the past few years." She shrugged. "But, I've missed you, too. I'm glad we'll be living in the same town now."

"Yeah, and working in the same building."

"Once again, how will people tell us apart?"

"You'll be in overalls and smelling like dirt, and I'll be wearing a chef's hat and smelling like fresh baked bread."

Evelyn laughed. It was good to be home. "Dad says the restaurant is doing well. I must admit I was skeptical about a restaurant above a plant nursery and landscaping business. I was worried about the manure deliveries in the spring."

"That has been a challenge. But, you know, Dad will do anything for us. He's paved a road to the back greenhouse and the poop is delivered there. You can still smell it from the entrance but it's dilute by then. A few aromatic shrubs on display at the door take care of it."

"Well, I'm just glad it worked so we can work together."

"Do you want a glass of wine?" Alice went into the kitchen and Evelyn followed.

"I'll drink one. I'd forgotten how far out we live from town. It took me half an hour to get here."

"Why don't you stay the night? You can run home in the morning. Nobody will be upset if you're not at work early. In fact, Dad said he was going to try to talk you into taking some time off."

"We've covered that."

"You aren't taking time off."

"No. But I do want to go home and spend the night in my own bed in my own room. I think I'd like to get up and help Dad with the horses, too." She winced remembering her mishap. She hoped Doris wasn't too traumatized. Elmo obviously didn't care at all.

Alice smiled as she handed her sister a glass of wine. "It is nice to hang out at home sometimes, isn't it?"

"Yeah. So, what do you hear about Jamie these days?"

"Jamie who?" Alice opened her eyes wide.

"You know Jamie who."

"Not James Parnell, Jr., your high school heart throb."

"I didn't go to high school with Jamie."

"That's right. He's quite a bit older than you. He must be pushing 30 by now."

"He has just turned 29. That's only five and a half years older than me. Mom's five years younger than Dad, so big deal."

"Kidding, kidding." Alice held up her hands. "I've always been on your side about that. I haven't heard much about Jamie lately. I know he's still working downtown at Georgia State University teaching tennis. I think the last I heard he'd been promoted from assistant coach to head coach. But he's not faculty yet."

"Is he, like, attached to anyone? I mean ...."

"I know what you mean. Honestly, Ev, I don't know."

"You work with his father's best friend. Surely you hear something about him from time to time."

"From time to time, but I don't ask. I'm sorry, Ev. I just don't think about it. He's your interest, not mine. I probably would have heard if he got married or something."

They sat down in the living area and passed a minute in silence. Each seemed lost in thought.

"So," Alice broke the silence. "You're still hung up on him."

"I love him so much. I tried dating other guys at school. It's just not going to happen. I hope I'm not too late."

"What happened with you and Jamie? You were so together before you went away to school."

"I don't know. He just changed. We planned a long-distance relationship. It isn't that long distance, so we saw each other a lot. Then he just cooled right off. At first, I was mad so I acted like I didn't care. I couldn't keep that up for long so I tried to talk to him."

"Didn't work?"

"He wouldn't talk. He started avoiding me." Evelyn got up and walked to the window. The drapes were pulled closed. She parted them and looked across the pond at the nursery. The sign was turned off, but she could see the letters Landrum's Nursery and Landscaping, a sign underneath said Alice's Café.

"Ev..."

"I don't believe he's stopped loving me, Al. I can't believe it."

"I'll talk to David."

"I'd appreciate it." She took a deep breath and smiled. "Well, do I get a tour of your apartment before I make the long drive home?"

*

Evelyn pulled into the parking lot of the family business the next day at about 11:00am. Alice was pulling in at about the same time.

"You're a little late, aren't you?" Alice said as she fell in beside Evelyn. "I thought you couldn't wait to get started."

"Dad wanted to introduce me to all the new rescue horses."

"By name, right?"

"Yes. It's nice that they do that. These poor horses have no other place to go. Since Mom and Dad don't ride anymore, they don't have to keep their own horses. I think this is as good for them as it is for the animals."

"They've got a couple of rescues that are ride-able. Did he tell you that?"

"Yeah, they're looking for homes for them. I guess they were found starving in a pasture somewhere. Once they were brought back to health, it was clear that they were young otherwise healthy horses. Dad says he's ridden both, but he can't give them the exercise they need. He wants us to do it."

"That would be fun. He's talked to me about it, too. We should do it. I haven't ridden in years." Alice opened the door and waved Evelyn inside.

"Hello, ladies."

They both looked up just in time to see their cousin, David, approaching, arms spread wide.

"David!" Evelyn cried as he swept them both into a bear hug consistent with the family tradition.

"I can't believe I've got both of you in my arms at the same time and I don't feel like I'm lifting anything." He put them down and kissed them each on the cheek. "Welcome to the family business. How am I going to tell you two apart since you have the same hair style?" He stood, crossed his arms, and studied the two of them.

"By the smell, David." Alice touched his arm and turned toward the stairs that led to the restaurant above.

He watched her go. "What does she mean by that?"

"I'm going to smell like manure, and she's going to smell like fresh baked bread."

"Oh," he laughed. "It's good to see you here. I have to go back upstairs. Alice and I share the lunch rush. I do breakfast. She's not a morning person."

"No, she's not. David," She stopped him before he left. "Are you as happy as Alice is with the restaurant business? I was a little unsure about you two being partners, and I wondered how you would feel about changing jobs at your age."

"Were you worried about the age difference?"

"Maybe a little."

"Were you worried she'd wear your old cousin out?"

"Alice wears me out."

"I know what you mean, but we're doing just fine. The energy is good for me." He hugged her again. "I'll stop by to see you before I go home. I'm so glad you're finally here for good." He took the stairs to the café two at a time then turned at the top and looked down at her. "Not bad for an old guy, huh?"

Evelyn laughed. Then she turned to look around her. The nursery opened into a big room sloping downhill for water runoff. In front, there were the checkout stations. Behind that to the right was the tropical plant section. There were four rows of indoor plants. There were shelves for pots and terrariums and hanging planters. There were shelves of decorative pebbles and mosses. To the left were sliding glass doors that opened to the landscape plants, perennials, annuals, shrubs and trees.

10 / Evelyn

Evelyn could feel the smile spreading over her face. She had grown up in this place. The smell of it was comfort. Her dad had brought them here to play in the dirt when they were babies, to plant their own gardens when they were kids, to work after school when they were teens, and now she would be carrying on the family business.

The door at the back of the building opened and Darcy, the office manager, came through it smiling, her arms open for a hug.

"There is my new associate," Darcy touched her shoulders in a semblance of a hug and made a mwa mwa noise next to her ear, a semblance of a kiss.

You'll start from the bottom and move up, Dad had said. Clearly Darcy planned to carry out his orders.

*

Later that afternoon Evelyn looked up at the sound of her father's voice. He approached her from the back of the building where the door led outside to a series of greenhouses. She stood up from the wheel barrow full of clay pots with which she was stocking the shelves.

"Come out to the potting shed. I want to show you some of the changes I've made." He draped his arm over her shoulder and started to guide her toward the door.

Evelyn pulled back and looked around. "I don't know, Dad. Darcy has a lot of other merchandise she wants me to stock. She didn't want me to take my break before I'm finished."

"Don't worry about that. I'm the boss remember."

It was tempting to let him overrule Darcy. He was in charge. But she was pretty sure that would be a strategic mistake. She fully intended to go to the top of this business, but she needed to approach it correctly or it would be difficult for all of them. Darcy had been with the place since Evelyn could remember, and even though she had never been very pleasant, she did a good job and she knew the business inside and out.

"Dad." She stood on her toes and kissed his cheek. "You said from the bottom up. The associates don't take their breaks until their supervisor tells them to. How about I come and get you when I can and you take me for a tour of the whole place. I think there are a number of new things to see."

He took a deep breath and studied her face. "I didn't mean you had to be a slave. You don't have to stock shelves." He looked around as the door to the shop opened and Darcy started in their direction.

"Dad." Evelyn put a restraining hand on his arm. "Let me do this my way. Please."

"Jeff," Darcy said as she approached. "I need to talk to you about another late order from the pebble supplier. This is the third late order. I had to go to another company. I think we need to think about not using them anymore." She looked at Evelyn. "Honey, I need these shelves stocked by the end of the day. You'll never take a break at this rate."

Evelyn squeezed her dad's arm as she felt him stiffen. He was full of big talk about starting from the bottom, but he was so soft on his daughters he'd never enforce it.

"Do you think you can handle the job, Evelyn?" Darcy continued. "Or should I get one of the part timers out of the potting shed to help you? I really can't spare either of them, but if you need someone ..."

"I can handle it, Darcy. I promise." She looked at her father's clenched jaw and pleaded with her eyes.

"Jeff, there are a couple of things I'd like to talk to you about. I'll meet you in the office." She turned, clearly unaware of the tension she had caused and walked briskly toward the office at the front of the nursery.

"Dad, go to the office and talk to Darcy. I'll come and get you when I reach a stopping point."

He clenched his jaw and looked at his manager's back as she crossed the room. "She's carrying this a bit too far."

"Dad, please don't say anything to her. I'll handle it."

He looked back at her and his eyes softened. "Okay, I'll try. Come and get me when you can."

"So, what was that all about?" Alice approached with two glasses of iced tea. Evelyn took one from her and drank about half of it.

"Darcy is throwing her weight."

"I think Dad should get rid of her now that you're here. She's such a bitch. I don't know how you'll stand her."

"I can learn a lot from her." Evelyn handed the glass back to Alice and grabbed a stack of clay pots out of the wheel barrow.

"Ev, you don't have to put up with her."

"Yes, I do. Let me do this my way." She didn't look at her sister as she climbed the step ladder to a higher shelf.

"Okay, have it your way. But if it goes too far, I'll talk to Dad."

"Please don't!"

Alice frowned and walked away. Evelyn watched her while climbing the ladder with a stack of clay pots in her hand. Suddenly she knocked her foot on the step and fell forward. Needing both hands to catch herself, she let the pots go. They crashed to the floor and broke into a thousand small pieces. She looked up. Darcy stood just outside the office door with her arms crossed. Jeff hurried around her to the ladder.

"Are you okay, honey?"

"I'm fine, Dad." She looked over his shoulder at Darcy who shook her head and went back into the office.

Chapter 2

Evelyn pulled her car into the parking lot at the tennis club where James Parnell, Jr. taught lessons. She had called his mother to say hello and to try to tactfully get an idea of where to find him. Apparently, he was teaching private lessons on the side to make extra money. This was a private club in a wealthy part of town. She'd managed to get a visitor's pass from the guard at the gate. Her convertible top was down, and she smilingly convinced him that she had forgotten her membership card, and her 'Daddy' would be furious if she was late for lunch.

She pulled into a parking space and looked around. Jamie was at the furthest court with a young student. A pretty girl with curly blond hair pulled into a knot on the top of her head. Just from the way she moved, Evelyn could tell she was only taking lessons to get close to the sexy tennis pro.

The lesson ended and the girl walked around the net to follow Jamie around the court while he gathered up balls. She was talking to him all the time. He answered her from time to time, and he turned to smile at her a couple of times. Evelyn could tell he was just being nice. He didn't seem interested. The two of them walked toward where she stood on the other side of the fence. Jamie was looking at the ground saying something to the girl. Then he looked up and stopped.

"Hey, Jamie," Evelyn called. The blond looked irritated, but Jamie seemed to have forgotten she was there. He just stood and stared.

"So, Jamie, you didn't answer me. Can you fit another lesson in this week? I really want to be a good tennis player." The blond was really pushing.

Jamie seemed to snap out of a daze. "I'll have to look at my schedule. I'll call you, Devon."

"Okay," Devon looked from one to the other of them. "Try, Jamie, please."

He hadn't stopped looking at Evelyn for a second. The girl walked away glancing over her shoulder, obviously annoyed.

"Hey, Jamie," Evelyn repeated.

"Evelyn." He walked through the gate and came to stand in front of her. "It's nice to see you. I heard you'd graduated."

"Yeah, I'm home for good now. I started at the nursery on Monday. After a lifetime of prep, I'm finally where I want to be."

"That's great." He smiled. It was a sad smile. "I'm happy for you. Well," He turned toward the clubhouse. "I've got to go. It was good to see you."

"Jamie, wait!" She hurried after him and put her hand on his arm. He stopped and looked down at her hand. He didn't meet her eyes. "I was hoping you were finished for the day. I thought we could have dinner, catch up with each other a little bit."

He took a deep breath. "I have another lesson this afternoon."

"What about afterwards?"

"No." He started walking toward the building again.

"Jamie, what's going on? Why do you hate me so much?"

His shoulders slumped. He took another deep breath and turned around. "I don't hate you, Evelyn. It's just over between us. It has been for a while. You have to accept that."

"Are you seeing Devon?" She was starting to get a very bad feeling.

He laughed. "She's seventeen years old."

"I was seventeen years old when you were dating me."

"That's right, and I was too old for you then. I'm definitely too old for a seventeen year old five years later."

"Are you seeing someone else?"

"Now and then."

"Now and then you see the same person? Or now and then you see different girls?"

"Evelyn, I really don't want to talk about this." He looked at his watch. "Look, I've got to go. I have a student in five minutes. I need some water before I start again."

"Tell me you don't love me anymore and I'll leave you alone." She put her hand on the door of her car to steady herself. She was struggling with a lump in her throat.

"Is that your car?" He asked.

She glanced around at the pale green Volkswagen bug with its convertible top down. "Yeah, Mom and Dad gave it to me for graduation."

"Wow, that's nice." There was something in the way he looked at the car that puzzled her. "But why didn't they get you a Porsche like they got Alice?"

"Alice bought it herself. Her restaurant is doing very well. She can buy her own car."

Jamie shook his head as if he was waking from a dream. He smiled, again sadly. "I'm sure you'll be able to buy your own car soon."

"When I can, I won't buy a Porsche." She laughed.

"No. You're the sensible twin." He turned to walk away. She ran after him and clutched his arm again.

"You didn't answer my question, Jamie. Do you still love me?"

He wiped his face with his towel and looked around the parking lot. "Look, Evelyn, I will always love you. I've known you all my life. We've been close. But the romantic relationship is over. It has to be. Now I've got to go." He shook her hand off his arm and walked quickly toward the building.

She turned to go back to the car. Not realizing she was standing in front of a bench she hit it with her knee and tumbled to the ground on the other side. She landed on her belly and rolled to her side.

"Damn it!" She said.

"Ev!" Jamie came to stoop beside her. "Are you alright?" He must have hurried back when he heard her fall. He took her elbow and tried to help her sit up.

"I'm fine!" She elbowed his hand away. "Just the same old Evelyn, clumsy and stupid."

"You're not stupid, Ev."

She looked at him and narrowed her eyes. "But I am clumsy."

"I'd be lying if I denied it."

He was stifling a smile. Maybe this had worked in her favor. She could take a little embarrassment if it would get her closer to Jamie.

"Look at you. You've scuffed yourself all up." He was looking at her knees.

"No, I did that the other day when I came home. I ..." She thought better of telling him of the car incident. "Well, I had another mishap."

This time he did laugh. Evelyn's heart thumped. He was so cute when he laughed.

"Well," He stood up and gathered his equipment off the bench. "Like I said, I'm running late. It was good to see you."

Just as he was turning to leave, a tennis ball flew over the fence and bounced off Evelyn's head. Jamie laughed, and shaking his head, he walked toward the clubhouse.

She watched him go. He was even more beautiful than she remembered him. Six feet two, broad shoulders, slim waist, his hair was a sandy blond and his eyes were a deep green. "I can't stop loving him. I can't." She murmured as she limped to her car.

*

"Do you remember how to saddle one of these things?" Alice asked.

"These things are horses and Dad said he'd help us. He said to get them out and brush them down until he got here." Evelyn looked at her sister and sighed. Her sister's short cap of dark hair had a piece of hay in it. She picked it out and threw it to the ground. "What made you cut your hair? It was all the way down to your waist."

"I don't know. I just wanted to, so I did. What's with you today? I haven't seen you so grumpy in years."

"Nothing!" Evelyn turned to the horse and started to brush him furiously.

"Hey," Jeff came into the barn and snatched the curry comb out of Evelyn's hand. "You're not supposed to attack him with it. You don't want to bruise him. What did he ever do to you?"

"She's seriously grumpy, Dad." Alice said. "Apparently she's mad at me for cutting my hair."

"I am too. Now I can't tell you two apart." Jeff laughed trying to lighten the mood. "You're going to have to start color coding yourselves like your mother used to."

"Oh, come on, Dad." Alice laughed. "Don't tell me you really can't tell us apart."

"I know you're Alice because I heard Evelyn ask you why you cut your hair. Otherwise it would be hard. After a few minutes with you I'd know. Your temperaments are very different."

"Especially today." Alice nodded her head at Evelyn's back and exchanged a look with her father.

"Are the horses ready to saddle?"

"Mine is," Evelyn said. "I'm sure Alice hasn't brushed her horse at all, what with her mouth going a hundred miles an hour."

"Ev, honey, you'll need to calm down. You don't want to spook the horse."

"The horse will be fine." She stalked to the tack room to get the saddle.

After Jeff had adjusted the stirrups for both girls they started down one of the familiar trails. There were twenty-five miles of trails in the area. They had lived there all their lives and they had always had horses.

Evelyn steadied her breathing and counted to ten. The feel of the horse's movements beneath her was soothing. She was beginning to feel a little better. "What did Dad say this horse's name was?" She asked.

"Well, since they were found abandoned in a pasture, they really didn't know their names. Dad and Mom decided to call them Roan and Dapple for their colors. That way you won't get them confused. I think the folks are getting a little flakey."

"I think you're right."

"Have you seen Jamie yet?"

"Yeah, I saw him yesterday. He said our romantic relationship was over."

"I'm sorry, Ev. I guess that's why you're feeling so out of sorts."

"That and other things." They walked in silence along the trail for a minute. "He's lying about his feelings. I could tell by the look on his face. I think he was shook up seeing me."

"Ev, are you sure you aren't beating a dead horse?"

"Shhhhh ... don't let Roan and Dapple hear you say something like that." They laughed. "Anyway, I asked him if he still loved me and he couldn't tell me he didn't. I'm not giving up."

"You always go after what you really want, and you usually get it. I'd just hate to see you get hurt."

"Look, Alice, we're on the flats beside the pond. Do you want to have a good run?"

"Yeah, let's see what these horses can do."

They ran across the field and up a path through the woods. It was late summer and in Georgia that's warm, but the horses didn't seem to mind. When they stopped they turned to go home.

"It seems like this ride has lightened your spirits a little bit."

"Yeah. You know, losing Jamie would hurt me more if I thought I didn't even try. I just don't understand what happened. We loved each other so much. I still love him that much."

"I know, Ev." Alice reached and put her hand on Evelyn's arm. "It was so romantic. I was envious. Maybe he found someone else while you were at school."

"I asked him. He was evasive. I don't think he has. I really think he still loves me. Maybe I'm just being stupid. But I think he still loves me."

"I hope so. Promise me something, though; promise you won't stop talking to me, even if you get your heart broken."

"Of course, I won't." Evelyn laughed. "When have I ever stopped talking to you?"

"Never."

"Do you know where Jamie lives, Al?"

"Not a clue."

"I think I'll pay his little sister a visit. I haven't seen her in ages."

"You weren't friends with Marisa. She's younger than us."

"I babysat for her. I'm sure she'll be glad to see me."

"You're ruthless, Ev. I love it!"

*

"Evelyn," Darcy came through the door of the green house. "We have a truck load of pine straw that needs to be unloaded. Go help the boys. It's a three-man job."

"I'm at a really critical point on these hybrids. I'd like to have them ready for the fall rush."

"Evelyn, I know hybridizing was one of your favorite classes in school. But you aren't in school anymore. Reality is frequently not as fun as the fantasy."

Evelyn counted to ten for the tenth time that day. She was trying to be patient with Darcy, but it was clear that she was being picked on. Darcy had never been a warm fuzzy person, but she'd always been civil. She had scolded her like a child a few days ago when she'd forgotten to open the nozzle on the hose.

"Darcy, I will be happy to help with the pine straw, but I can't stop what I'm doing right now or I'll ruin the hybrids. Ask Jason to get started without me. I'll be there in ten minutes."

Darcy crossed her arms and glared. "It seems to me that you have forgotten who the supervisor is around here. Your father was very clear about you learning the business from the bottom up. And that is what I intend to teach you."

"My father has great respect for the plants and flowers that we cultivate here. I'm sure he wouldn't approve of half finishing a job when the result will be losing the plants."

Darcy huffed. "Are you threatening me?"

"No, ma'am. I just want to finish what I've started. Then I'll help with the other things that need to be done."

Darcy glared for a minute. Then she left the green house, brushing past David as she went.

"That was great." David sat down on a stool beside her. "She sure is swinging her weight with you. Alice says she's being a slave driver. You know, Uncle Jeff would put a stop to that very quickly if you asked him to."

"I know." She sniffed and wiped a tear from her cheek. "I wanted to handle it myself, but I hate confrontation. I'm not doing a very good job."

"Hey." He put his arm across her shoulders. "You've always been the quiet one. But you've also always been the one who knew exactly what she wanted to do."

"I didn't want to do this. I didn't want to have to fight my way into the business."

"You don't have to and you know it." He squeezed her shoulder. "I'm sure you've thought about it, but look at Darcy's position. She's worked here for something like twenty-five years. Then along comes the boss's daughter, all educated and ready to take over."

"I'm not trying to take over."

"I know you're not, at least not yet."

Evelyn laughed.

"But I'm sure Darcy is feeling very insecure right now."

"I guess you're right, but what do I do about it. I'm not after her job. I know this place is her life. I mean how many times has she been married in the last twenty-five years, two, three? They never worked, and Mom always said it was because she was married to the nursery. There wasn't room for a husband."

"I think she's probably right."

"So, what do I do, David? I've been here for three weeks. It's been one battle after another with her. She doesn't want me to do anything but physical labor like stock shelves and unload pine straw. Yesterday she had me bagging compost. It isn't that I'm above doing that stuff, but I want to do other stuff too. Like this." She pointed to the plants she was working on. "Even the part time kids get to make terrariums and hanging baskets. I had to sneak in here on my break to do this."

"I don't know how to handle it, but I have faith that you'll figure it out."

"Thanks a bunch!"

"Anyway, the reason I'm here is because Alice sent me to get you for lunch. It's 1:30 and you need to eat something."

"I can't. I have to finish this and go outside to unload the pine straw."

"The boys have done it. Finish up here and come on up. We have a great salad on special, Thai noodle. Great for a hot day like today."

"Okay." Just as David was opening the door to leave Evelyn said, "Do you know where Jamie lives? You're his Dad's best friend. Has he told you where he lives?"

"He moved recently. He was living in an apartment near the campus, but he doesn't live there anymore. I don't know where he does live, though. Why?"

"I just wondered."

"Sorry I couldn't help."

*

Evelyn sat on the stone bench beside the goldfish pond in her parent's yard. Her mother's Rottweiler sat at her feet. They'd always had one. It made her mother feel safe. Evelyn had never known what Amanda needed to be protected from. Nobody had, but they had all loved the succession of the big dogs. There was a greyhound sleeping in a straw bed under an apple tree. All the dogs were rescues. They were such good people. Evelyn had always felt like she just didn't quite fit in. Alice was so strong willed and hot tempered. Her dad was hot tempered too, but fair. No matter how mad he was, he could always see reason. Mom was so gentle but still so strong.

"Here I am wanting to give up, Lou Lou." She rubbed the big dog's soft head. "None of them ever wanted to give up. Dad loves to tell the story of how Mom didn't want anything to do with him, but he didn't give up until she agreed to marry him. Dad says Mom had a bad childhood. She doesn't even talk about it but she didn't give up. Alice didn't want to go to college like she was supposed to. She wanted to have her own restaurant. Now she does.

"I can't get anything I want. I'm not ever going to get where I want to go in the business, not with Darcy in the way. And Jamie won't have anything to do with me. I can't even find him. And I'm so clumsy, I'd better not get any closer to the pond or I'll fall in and scare the fish."

She smiled at the thought and looked down into Lou Lou's big liquid brown eyes. "You're a great dog, Lou." The greyhound nudged her from behind. She turned to stroke his boney head and his muscular neck. "You are a lazy bum, Arthur." She put her arms around his neck and rested her head on his shoulder.

*

"Over here, Marisa." Evelyn waved from the booth in the corner of the café where she was meeting Jamie's younger sister. The girl saw her and headed over. Evelyn stood and hugged her.

"I was so surprised when you called to invite me to lunch. It's been such a long time since we've done anything together." Marisa sat down at the table. "Have you ordered anything?"

"No, I was waiting for you. How have you been? Are you in school? I can't believe I don't know this stuff. It's not like I've been out of the country or anything."

"Well, you have been focusing on school. I know how that is. I'm in my third year at Georgia State. If you're trying to get out in good time, you don't have a lot of time to socialize."

"Wow, I didn't realize you were that far along in school." Evelyn picked up her menu. She hoped she didn't seem nervous. She hoped Marisa couldn't see through the pretense of being interested in her. Not that she didn't like the girl. "What are you studying?"

"I'm pre-med. I'm hopeful. My grades are good. I expect I'll find a Medical school that will take me."

"That's great. Where do you want to go to Medical school?"

"I'll apply to several, but Emory is my first choice. I love Atlanta, and I want to stay close to my family, and ..." She looked at her menu. "I have a boyfriend."

"Really, anybody I know?"

"I doubt it. His name is Mike Allen. I met him at school. He isn't from Atlanta, but he plans to stay here after he graduates. He's a graduate student, and he already has a position in the athletic department."

"The athletic department at Georgia State?" Evelyn's heart began to pound. "Does he know your brother?"

"He does. That's how we met. They're friends. He brought him to the house for dinner one time. I think it really was love at first sight, if you believe in that kind of thing."

"I do."

"Of course, Jamie was all protective of me. He was really mad at Mike for a while. He said he's too old for me. Of course, you know that's silly. Mike is only four years older than me. Jamie is six years older than you."

"Five and a half." Evelyn couldn't think. The waitress came to the table. She wasn't even sure what she ordered.

"So, Ev, I really like you and all, but we both know why you invited me to lunch."

"What do you mean?" Evelyn tried to cover, then dropped her chin to her chest. "I'm sorry, Marisa. It's just, I don't know what to do next. I just can't believe it's over. I won't believe it's over."

"Ev." Marisa reached across the table to touch her arm. "I don't think it's over for him either. I don't know what happened. It seemed like he loved you so much. Then suddenly he told us you had broken up and he didn't want to talk about it. At first, I figured you had found someone else at school. I knew he wasn't seeing anyone else."

Evelyn looked up. "He isn't?"

"No."

"Are you sure?"

"Yes."

"So, what's the problem?"

"Beats me. But I can tell you where to find him."

"You can ... and you will?"

"Sure. He and Mike eat lunch every day at the school cafeteria. They have a staff pass. It doesn't cost them anything. The food isn't bad. Mike is eating lunch with me on Friday, so Jamie will eat alone. They always go at noon on the dot."

"What if he decides to skip it?"

"Then he won't be there, but I don't think he'll skip it. Do you remember Jamie's appetite?"

"I'm off on Friday. I work Saturday this week. That's perfect. Thanks, Marisa." She looked down at the sandwich she had ordered, suddenly feeling hungrier than she had in a while. "I'm sorry about the pretense. You know I am interested in you. I've always liked you."

"Don't worry about it. Like I said, I'm in love, too. I'd die if Mike didn't want to see me anymore."

"Where does Jamie live, Marisa?"

"That, I can't help you with. He won't tell us. I'm pretty sure Mom knows, but she's pretty good at keeping a secret. I don't even think Dad knows."

"That is so strange."

Chapter 3

Evelyn felt a twinge of nostalgia as she entered the school cafeteria. She'd eaten at the University of Georgia cafeteria many times in the five years she had attended the school. She looked around the crowded room and zeroed in on Jamie. He sat across from a very attractive redhead in the far corner. He was smiling at something she was saying. She felt a twinge of something between anger and fear. Maybe he was seeing someone. Maybe she was too late.

She paused for a minute to let her galloping pulse slow to normal then breathed in to the count of four, exhaled to the count of four, and proceeded across the room.

"Hello, Jamie." He jumped and looked up at her.

"Evelyn, what are you doing here?"

"I came to see you." She had thought of a very good excuse for being there, but she couldn't use it. He needed to know the truth.

"Well, it's about time for me to be getting back to work."

"I thought you took an hour at noon. That's what Marisa told me."

His jaw clenched. She smiled. He always clenched his jaw when something irritated him. She hoped she hadn't gotten Marisa in too much trouble.

"Okay," he said. "Would you like to join us?" He pointed to the chair that she stood behind.

"I have to go, Jamie." The redhead stood and picked up her tray.

"I'm sorry, Helen. This is a friend of mine, Evelyn Landrum. Evelyn, this is Helen Morris. She's a co-worker of mine."

"It's nice to meet you." Helen said. "I'd shake your hand, but I'm overloaded."

"That's okay. It's nice to meet you, too."

Evelyn sat down resisting the urge to be upset as Jamie watched Helen leave the cafeteria. "Are you dating her?" She was startled by her own question.

Jamie looked back at her. He was clearly thinking his answer through. He always wore his feelings on his face. Even though he was older, he was so innocent, so real. He couldn't lie if he wanted to.

"We've been out a couple of times."

"Oh." She knew he wasn't lying. She could also tell he had no romantic feelings for Helen.

"Why are you here, Evelyn?"

"Because I can't seem to see you any other way, and I really want to see you. Jamie, just tell me what's wrong. Tell me why you don't love me anymore. I can't just let this go if I don't even know why. I've never stopped loving you. I never will."

He covered his face with both hands and rubbed his eyes. "Evelyn, it just won't work. I'm six years older than you, and …"

"Five and a half."

He looked at her and almost smiled. "Close enough. I cringe when I think of how many times I promised your dad I wouldn't take advantage of your innocence. I broke that promise."

"I think it was more like me taking advantage of your innocence, and I didn't make my dad any promises." She laughed, and she saw the struggle Jamie had not to smile at her. "Jamie, please don't tell me you're going to throw away what we had, what we have, because you feel guilty about making love to me. I don't regret it for a second, and Dad never has to know."

"You were seventeen years old. That's statutory rape."

"I was two weeks away from my eighteenth birthday. If we'd waited two weeks would you feel better about it?"

He gathered his plates and flatware onto his tray, obviously making a point not to look at her. "That isn't what matters, Evelyn. It's just over. I guess I don't regret it, but it's still over. Once you get going in your career, you'll meet someone you have more in common with. I'm surprised you didn't meet someone at school. I thought you would."

"I met lots of people at school. I even dated a little. They weren't you."

"Evelyn, it was an infatuation. You were young. I paid attention to you. Let it go. I have."

Fighting a lump in her throat the size of Stone Mountain, she blinked her eyes. So far, the tears hadn't run over, but she knew her eyes were swimming. "Have you really let it go, Jamie? Can you really let me go?"

He looked at her, then away. "I have to go back to work." He looked her in the eyes. "Evelyn, I'm sorry. I really am." He stood and walked away from her.

She stared at the table and wondered if she would get out of the cafeteria without bursting into tears.

*

Saturday was hard. Evelyn didn't have to be in until noon, which gave her time to soak her tear stained face in ice water until she looked almost normal. Her parents were conspicuously silent at the breakfast table where she pushed some food around on her plate. She couldn't even remember what it was.

She insisted on feeding the rescued horses while Jeff fed Doris and Elmo. They usually worked together. She needed the time alone with the animals today.

Lou Lou accompanied her to the rescue pasture while Arthur went with her father. He rarely left his side. She opened the barn door and went in. There were four horses in the barn. One was too old to ride. He was a thirty-two-year-old white Arab, who looked surprisingly good for his years. The owners didn't want him anymore so they called the rescue service. How could people do that? If they'd loved him when he was useful why didn't they love him now?

"I guess Jamie would understand. Wouldn't he, Dancer?" She stroked the soft muzzle. She fed him a carrot then scooped a can of grain out of the bucket to pour into his trough.

"Good morning, Francie." Just the contact with the horses and the dog was helping. Francie a chestnut mare of about twenty had gone lame and was unable to be ridden. She had been found tied to a fence post at the local humane society. Both of them would live their lives out in luxury with her parents. She cringed to think of all the poor unfortunates that wouldn't. She poured a scoop of grain into her trough and moved along to Roan and Dapple.

Roan danced happily at her approach and Dapple uttered a low whicker. "You guys are ready to get out and stretch your legs a little bit, aren't you?" She gave them their grain then went to the stall where they kept the hay. Dragging a bail off the top of the pile, she cut the strings and picked it up in handfuls to shake loose in the hay trough.

"Is everyone finished?" She turned back to the horses and one by one opened the stall doors to release them to the pasture for the day.

"I guess that's it, Lou Lou." She stroked the soft head of the Rottweiler. "I feel better." She sighed. "I guess life goes on."

"Animals work wonders, Mom." She said as she let herself into the kitchen. "I feel so much better."

"I'm glad, honey."

Amanda never pried into her daughters' affairs. But they both knew she was there to listen if they wanted to talk.

"Why don't we have any cats, Mom? I've never known you to be without a cat."

"Blue died last month. The last year was rough with his diabetes and all. I thought I'd just take a break."

"Are you okay? I've never known you to want a break from your pets."

"Just a little tired. I've loved them all, but I've lost so many. Sometimes you just wonder how many times you grieve without crumbling."

Evelyn felt her pulse quicken. Her mother had never talked like that.

"Anyway," Amanda turned and smiled at her daughter. "I was thinking we'd start with barn cats. Jeb died about a month after Blue and the barns are getting overrun with rats and mice. What do you say we go to the humane society and pick out a few that look outdoorsy? You know my barn cats live in luxury, too."

"That sounds great. Tomorrow is Sunday. The nursery is closed, although when I'm in charge I'm going to change that."

Amanda smiled at her daughter's enthusiasm. She was relieved that the mood of the morning had lifted. "Let's go tomorrow then. Maybe Alice would like to come with us."

"Maybe Dad will come, too. We'll make it a family outing." Evelyn said. "I've got to go get dressed now or I'll be late for work."

*

"How was work today, Ev?" Evelyn and Alice were sitting in the kitchen of the café sipping a glass of wine. Alice insisted on managing the Saturday night dinner shift. She had a manager that could handle it, but Saturday was such an important night that she couldn't relax unless she was there. No reason for both of them to be there.

"It was great. Darcy was off today."

"Who supervised you? As if anybody needs to supervise you."

"Dad supervised everyone else. I was pretty much on my own. I know I'm trying not to take advantage of my status as the owner's daughter. But it's nice to be able to do some of the things I want to do in the place. It's not like I goofed off or anything. There was a lot that needed to be done in the green houses. They've been a bit neglected since Dad's partner retired. Well not the plants of course. Dad wouldn't let that happen. But the upkeep of the greenhouses themselves, Victoria pretty much ran that part of the business."

"I was glad she sold Dad back her portion of the business." Alice said. "It was great for him to have a partner, and she was a great partner. She was there just when he needed it, but I'm glad the business has come back into the family."

"I am too, especially since I intend to work my way up to the top. I'm going to run this place someday."

"Nobody doubts that."

"I think Darcy does. But I'll make her see. And I'll do it diplomatically."

"See, that's the difference between you and me. You want to do all this diplomatically. You don't want to use Dad's influence to get things your way. I, on the other hand, have no problem with letting Dad pave the way for me."

"Al, all you've ever cared about is getting your way."

"Well, that's important, isn't it?

Evelyn laughed and sipped her wine. "I'm worried about Mom."

"Why?" Alice sat up straight and looked at her sister with concern.

"She doesn't have a cat."

Alice sat back and laughed. "She has five horses, a mule, and two dogs. She's not exactly deprived of animal company."

"I know, but can you remember a time when she didn't have a cat? I asked her this morning why, and she said she was tired, needed a break."

"Blue's death was hard on her. I've never seen her take so long to recover."

"She said she doesn't know how many losses she can take before she crumbles."

"You don't suppose she's getting depressed, do you?"

"I don't know but Mom is such a private person. I'm not sure we'd know if she was." Evelyn finished her wine.

"Another glass?" Alice held up the bottle.

"No, it's a long way home. One glass is enough. Listen, she wants to go and get some barn cats from the shelter tomorrow. Come with us. Maybe we can talk her into a kitten. You know she can't resist a kitten."

"Okay, I'll be out there about noon."

"See you then."

*

Evelyn watched Alice's pink Porsche glide down the driveway. She sat in the loft of the rescue barn, her legs dangling out the window. She'd gone down to feed early. She wanted to make sure there was a proper place for the new cats they would bring home. They had always made beds in the tack room on the ground floor, but today she'd wanted to scout out the loft.

She remembered playing there when she was a kid. The loft was full of fond memories. The truth was, that's why she'd wanted to come up here. She and Alice had played there together when they were small. It was their playhouse. They had put their toy kitchen in the corner. They had stacked the straw that was kept for bedding to make walls. Evelyn smiled at the memory.

She had tasted her first beer up there. She'd been smart, though. Alice drank too much and puked out the window in the back of the barn. She still didn't like beer. Evelyn had only drunk one. She could still enjoy the bubbly freshness of an ice cold beer.

She'd smoked her first cigarette up here. Idiot! She thought, as she looked around at the dry straw all over the loft. We're lucky we didn't burn the place down. She shuddered at the memory of herself puking out of the back window. She'd never smoked another cigarette.

She sighed and looked at the cozy corner in the end of the loft where she and Jamie had both lost their virginity. Fighting a lump in her throat, she stood and went to meet Alice at the house.

"Well, did you get good beds made up for the new family members?" Jeff asked when she got to the house.

"Yeah. I was thinking maybe the loft would be a better place for them, but I was wrong. The tack room is definitely better. It's heated. They won't be cold in the winter." Evelyn said.

Of course, they'll live in the tack room, Ev," Alice said. "I don't know what you were thinking." The expression on her face said that she did know what she was thinking.

"Well, you have to check things out."

"Shall we go?" Amanda said as she came into the room.

"All set." Jeff guided the women into the garage where they all piled into the car.

When they arrived at the shelter, Alice jumped out of the car. She was the first one into the room where they kept the cats. She was always the first one. Alice never changed.

"Look, Mom," she called from across the room. "You've got to see these kittens. It's a whole litter, six of them. Mom, they're all white except one of them has a black tail."

"I'm not interested in kittens, Alice. You can't put kittens out in a barn and expect them to survive." She turned to speak to the attendant. Alice exchanged a look with Evelyn.

"She wouldn't even look at them," Alice whispered to Evelyn when she joined her at the cage with the kittens. "That's scary. I think you're right, Ev. She is depressed."

"What are the two of you whispering about over here?" Jeff asked. "Are you plotting to bring home a new kitten?"

"Dad," Evelyn said. "We don't have to plot. We're grown women, remember."

"No way." He smiled and put his hands on their shoulders. "So what's the buzzing about?"

"Dad, we're worried about Mom. I've never seen her not even want to look at kittens."

"Alice is right. Think back, Dad. Has Mom ever lived without a cat? She hasn't since we were born. What about before that."

Jeff's face registered concern. "No, she's always had one." He looked across the room at his wife. "Why doesn't she want a kitten?"

"I think she's depressed, Dad."

"Depressed? She's not the one that gets depressed. That's usually me." He hurried across the room to Amanda. Alice and Evelyn watched him say something to her and point in the direction of the cage full of kittens. She shook her head and followed the attendant to another cage. Jeff walked behind still talking and pointing in their direction.

"We'd better go over there. He's going to get on her nerves."

"Look here, girls." Amanda pointed to a cage with two large tabbies. One was orange and the other a silvery color. "John says that these are tamed feral cats. You know, wild. He says they'll probably never be happy in someone's house. I think that's perfect, don't you?"

"Yeah," Evelyn said reluctantly. "I guess that's pretty much what you want in a barn cat."

"Can you touch them?" Alice asked the attendant.

"Sure, they're pretty tame. I've worked with them some, but most of the socializing was done by another guy that works here. Well, I mean, he volunteers. He's spent hours and hours with them."

He opened the cage and gently pulled the silver tabby out. "You just have to move slowly with them. Do you want to hold her?" He extended the cat to Amanda.

"No!" She stepped back to avoid contact. Alice and Evelyn exchanged a look with their father this time. He was obviously worried.

"I want to hold her." Alice stepped forward.

Evelyn reached into the cage and gently pulled the orange tabby into her arms. "I guess this is a male. Aren't most orange cats males?"

"Most of them." The attendant stroked the cat's head. "This one is, but we see the occasional orange female.

"Are they spayed and neutered?" Amanda asked, all business.

"Yes, ma'am. They've had their shots and been tested for Feline Leukemia and Aids. They're all set for adoption. I think they'd make perfect barn cats. They will need some human contact, though. You don't want them to go back to being wild."

Amanda turned and headed for the adoption desk. "We have carriers in the car. Jeff, will you get them while I start the adoption process?"

"Don't you want to even look at the kittens, Manda? You love kittens."

"No!" Her answer was so final. Jeff looked at the girls, shrugged, and left the building.

The attendant went behind the counter to get the paperwork. A couple with a little girl had been looking around the room. They asked him to open the cage with the kittens so the child could hold one.

"I'll be right there," he said to the woman. "Let me get the guy in the back to help you adopt these guys. He'll be glad to know they have a home. He's the one that tamed them."

He disappeared through a door and returned a minute later with none other than James Parnel, Jr. Evelyn sucked in her breath.

"Well, Jamie," Amanda said. "What an unexpected surprise. How long have you worked here?"

"For a while." He looked at Evelyn and blushed. "I don't actually work here. I volunteer. I'm still working at the university."

"Well, that's nice. I understand you tamed the two cats we're taking for our barn."

"Yes ma'am. A barn is the perfect place for them. I don't think you could keep them in a house. I know they'll be happy in your barn. It's a great place."

Evelyn smiled at him knowingly. He blushed and turned away.

"Hello, James," Jeff said as he put the carriers on the desk. He shook Jamie's hand.

"Hello, Mr. Landrum. You'd better let me put the cats in the carriers. They don't like small places. You'll probably never get them back into one of these things."

"That's okay," Alice said. "Mom and Dad have a vet that comes to the house for the horses. He's always treated our cats and dogs, too."

Jamie loaded the cats into the boxes while Amanda filled out the paperwork and paid for them. He helped carry them out to the car and said goodbye. Evelyn watched him turn and walk back to the building.

"Wait a minute," she said to her family. "I'll be right back." She hurried after him. "Jamie, wait."

He stopped and fisted his hands by his sides. He didn't turn around for a minute but then he turned slowly and smiled reluctantly.

"I think I want to adopt one of those white kittens. I'm moving into my own apartment next week. It's over there across from the nursery. You'll have to come and see it once I get settled."

"Did you have your eye on any particular one?" He didn't respond to her invitation.

"Any particular what? Oh, kitten. Well." She moved over to the cage to look. "Can I take them out?"

"Sure." He opened the cage, and she reached in to pull out the white one with the black tail. She snuggled the tiny creature up to her face and smiled. She did love kittens. She was an animal lover like her mother.

"A kitten is exactly what my new apartment needs. He'll make it a home." She looked up at Jamie. He had a warm smile on his face which he quickly erased. Her heart fluttered. He did still have feelings for her. He was trying to hide them. Why?

"That one is a spitfire. You might rather have one of the others."

"No, this is the one I want. She held the kitten a few inches from her face and smiled. The little cat purred. Evelyn smiled. Then the creature took a swing at her face and landed two scratches right across her nose.

"Ev!" Jamie grabbed the kitten and put it back in the cage with its litter mates. "Are you okay?" He took her face in his hands and examined her nose.

She smiled absently. I sure am glad he scratched me, she thought. "I'm okay, Jamie." She felt something running down her nose to her cheek. She knew it was blood and wiped it off with the back of her hand.

"Come into the office. I'll clean that up."

"Okay."

"Sit down." He motioned to the chair in front of the desk. "I'll get the first aid kit."

"Okay." She couldn't seem to say anything else.

He cleaned the scratches with a gauze square. "This is going to sting," he said as he tore open an antiseptic pad.

"Okay." She said again then winced when he touched it to her wounds.

"Leave it to you to get injured holding a kitten." He laughed. He looked at her and stopped laughing abruptly. "Maybe you should choose another kitten. The others are really sweet."

"No, that's the kitten I want." She would be forever grateful to the little cat.

"Ev, he isn't going to get any better."

"I don't care. That's the kitten I want. I hate to leave the others, though. What happens if they don't get homes?"

"They'll get homes." He applied a band aid to her nose and stood back to look at her. "That's my Ev." He laughed again and straightened his features quickly.

She adopted the kitten and loaded him into a cardboard box. "Jamie, let me have your phone number. When I get settled I'll have you over for dinner."

"Uhmm ... I don't know, Evelyn. I'm pretty busy these days."

"You have to eat dinner. Come on. Give me your number. What are you afraid of? I'm not going to attack you or anything."

"I'm not afraid of anything. I just have a lot going on."

"Please give me the number."

He reached for a post it and scribbled a number on it. Then he turned and disappeared through the door to the office. Evelyn smiled and picked up the box. She was making progress.

"What happened to you?" Jeff said when she got to the car.

"Nothing." She grinned and got into the back seat.

*

"Evelyn!" She cringed as Darcy's voice intruded on her thoughts. "You've been sitting on that bail of pine straw for half an hour. Those bails won't stack themselves, you know."

Evelyn took a deep breath. She seemed to take a lot of deep breaths these days, at least while she was at work. "Darcy, I was taking a break. If you'll notice, I'm almost finished here."

"I don't remember telling you that your breaks were half an hour long."

"It hasn't been half an hour. Why are you being so hard on me? I've known you all my life. I don't remember you being so mean."

Darcy seemed to hesitate at this, but only for a few seconds. "I'm not mean, Evelyn. I'm your supervisor, and if you're going to spend all your time daydreaming I'll need to hire someone else."

"What's the problem?" Jeff asked as he came through the door to the yard. Darcy jumped, startled, and turned around to face him.

"There isn't a problem, Dad." Evelyn spoke quickly. His interference at this point would only make things worse.

"Are you sure?" He scowled at Darcy.

"Evelyn was taking a break," Darcy said. "I think she lost track of time."

"That's right, Dad. I was off in space." She laughed. "Thanks, Darcy. I need to get back to work now." She picked up the bail of straw by the twine holding it together and put it on top of the stack.

"Honey," Jeff picked up the next bail before she got to it. "You're too small to do this stuff. Let Jason do that." He tossed the bail onto the top of the stack. "Darcy, why don't you get Jason to do this?"

"Dad." She put her hand on his arm and looked at him, willing him with her eyes not to interfere. "Remember, I told you I wanted to do every part of the business. I studied that in school. I told you about it at the time. You shouldn't ask your employees to do anything you wouldn't do or haven't done." She held his eyes with hers for just a second then went back to stacking the bails.

"Well, be careful with your back. You're going to need it for a lot of years yet."

"I know my limits, Dad, and I've had all the safety courses you put all your employees through. Trust me. I'll be fine."

He took a deep breath and looked at Darcy. She had this way of making people breathe deeply.

"I'd like to see you in the office, Darcy. Have you got a minute?"

"Of course."

Evelyn watched them walk back to the building. Oh, she hoped he wasn't going to get involved in whatever was going on between her and Darcy. Well, if he did, she'd deal with it.

She finished stacking the straw and went into the greenhouse to wash her hands. There was a whole row of seedlings to replant. Some of them were put out in their seed trays and sold by the flat. But others were put into larger pots and sold separately for a slightly higher price. Then some others were put into terrariums and baskets for sale in the garden shop.

Evelyn loved that part of the job. She could spend all day in the greenhouse burying her fingers in the dirt and sifting through the sand. She loved seeing the arrangements come together and watching the plants in the terrariums start to thrive. She took a few minutes to do some repotting. After all, it had to get done, right?"

"I don't remember telling you to work in here?" Darcy's voice broke into her thoughts again. Her tone was clearly hostile. Dad had probably said something to her.

"I'm sorry, Darcy. I just thought as long as I was here … but, no, you're right. I should have waited for you to tell me what to do next." She threw the gardening gloves she had been using into the dirty glove box and washed her hands again. She turned to face Darcy.

She was startled by the look on Darcy's face. It wasn't anger. What was it? Hurt? Fear? "Darcy?" Evelyn stepped forward and put her hand on the woman's arm.

Darcy looked down at the hand on her arm. She stood like that for a few seconds. Then she said, "I'll need you on the checkout line, Evelyn. One of our cashiers is sick." She turned and walked out of the greenhouse, dropping Evelyn's hand to her side.

The checkout line was not her favorite part of the business. The truth was she wasn't very good at it. But you've got to do what you've got to do. She went to the office for the money drawer. Jeff wasn't there. She was glad. The situation needed some cooling off. Darcy handed her the drawer without saying a word. She went to her register and started the process of opening it up. There weren't very many people in the place at that moment, so there was no hurry.

The jingle of the bells on the front door signaled the entrance of a customer, and Evelyn looked up to greet them.

"Hello, Oh!" She recognized the redheaded women she'd met when she went to the university to see Jamie. "Helen, isn't it? I don't know if you remember me. I'm …"

"I remember. You're Jamie's friend. You know, I knew the name Landrum sounded familiar to me. This is one of my favorite places in the world. I'm an avid gardener. I guess you're related to the owner in some way?"

"Yeah, he's my dad."

"And you're following in his footsteps. How nice. I'm sure he's pleased."

"I think he's happy about it."

"Good, well I'm going to get one of the little red wagons over here and fill it up. I have the afternoon off today, and I plan to spend all of it playing in the dirt."

"Good for you." Evelyn watched as she walked away pulling the wagon. She sure is a pretty lady, she thought. She wondered how many times she and Jamie had gone out. Had Jamie kissed her? Had they …? No, don't even think about that. Think about work. She turned back to the checkout where a small line had formed and smiled at the next customer.

"I almost had to get another wagon." Helen laughed as she pulled the loaded cart up to the check out. "At a point, I have to remind myself of how much I can actually do in an afternoon. I swear. I could buy the place out."

"That's what we like to hear."

"So, have you known Jamie for long?" Helen asked as she put the seed packets on the counter.

Evelyn began scanning the plants in the wagon. She hoped she looked disinterested. "I've known him all my life. His dad was my cousin's best friend. My cousin is more like a brother to me. He's a lot older, but we're close."

"That's nice. So you and Jamie have been friends for a long time." She paused as if she wanted to say more. "I know it's none of my business, but was it something more than friendship?"

Evelyn looked up, startled. "Why do you ask that?"

"I just thought I might be picking up on some kind of undercurrent when we met at the school."

"We did go out for a while. I … I know you've dated him some, and …"

"You know I've … No, Evelyn, Jamie and I haven't dated."

"You haven't! He told me you'd been out a few times."

"Well, technically that's true. We've had dinner and once we went to a movie, Jamie, me, and my husband Don."

"Your husband?" Evelyn could feel the dawning smile on her face.

"Yes, we're all friends. We all work in the athletic department at the school. I'm an exercise physiologist. Don is, too. I also have a degree in nutrition. We coach the student athletes. Jamie and Don watch college football together in the fall and whatever other sport is going on at whatever time of the year. He's great with Damon, our son."

"You have a son?"

"Yes, uh oh," Helen looked at the woman waiting behind her. "We need to move along. You're forming a line."

"Oh no," Evelyn looked at the scanner in her hand. "I can't remember which ones I've scanned and which ones I haven't. I'm terrible at this job."

"You stopped here." Helen pointed to one of the plants. Evelyn finished checking her out and started on the next customer.

"Maybe we could all four go out sometime." Helen called from the door.

"That would be great!" The smile on her face was so broad it hurt. They'd gone out a few times. It was the closest Jamie could come to a lie.

*

Evelyn picked up the small cat by the scruff and guided him butt first into the plastic carrier she'd bought. The little creature hissed and growled his displeasure and took a swing at her hand as she pulled it out and closed the door.

"I don't know why you wanted that kitten," her mother said. "He scratched you before you even adopted him."

"He needs me, Mom. Nobody else will want him. Besides, ever since that first scratch, he's kept his claws retracted when he swats me. I think he's fallen for me."

"Well," Amanda turned to look out the kitchen window. "I'm not glad you're moving out, but I'm glad he is."

"Oh, come on, I saw you stroking him when he fell asleep in your lap last night."

"Habit."

She didn't turn from the window. Evelyn put the carrier down on the kitchen table and went to stand beside her. She put her arms around her shoulders. There were tears in Amanda's eyes. One spilled over and ran down her cheek. She dashed it away with the back of her hand and turned to take her daughter in her arms.

"Mom, please don't be so sad. I won't be a stranger. I promise I'll come to dinner every Sunday, and Alice and I are planning to ride on Fridays. We both have Fridays off."

"I'm sorry. I know you have to go. You just have to put up with a mother's tears, I guess. I never thought of myself as the weepy type."

"You've never been the weepy type. That's why I'm worried about you. Mom, I think you might be a little bit depressed."

"That's ridiculous." She pulled away and bent to look into the carrier. "Goodbye, bad news," she said to the kitten. "I can't believe you named him Sugar. He really isn't sweet."

"He is too sweet. You should see him at night. He wraps his paws around my neck, buries his head under my chin and sucks his thumb. Now that's sweet. That was very smooth the way you changed the subject, but it won't work. I'm not finished. I think it would help you to talk about how you're feeling."

"There is nothing to talk about." She straightened and looked back at Evelyn. "And I'd appreciate it if you wouldn't talk to your dad about it either. He's looking at me strangely these days. Like he's afraid I'm going to fall apart or something. He's helping me around the house and giving me gifts. He bought me a diamond ring. He's even suggested we get married again."

"You're kidding!"

"No. I wasn't that crazy about the first wedding. I sure don't want to have another one."

"You didn't like your wedding? You never told me that."

"I like my marriage, of course. But I don't like being the center of attention. It was okay. It was small. We were surrounded by friends, but I'd have rather just gone to the justice of the peace."

"I know what you mean about being the center of attention. I've never liked it either."

"No," Amanda smiled. "You always hid behind Alice at your birthday parties. I don't think you ever blew out a single candle."

"No, but it worked out fine. Alice loves being the center of attention, and she was always more full of hot air than me, too."

They both laughed for a minute. Then they just looked at each other. Amanda's eyes filled with tears again. Evelyn put her arms around her and they held each other for a moment. Nobody spoke.

"What's going on?" Alice's voice broke the spell and they moved apart.

"I'm just having a little trouble letting my youngest go." Amanda laughed and blotted her eyes with a dish towel.

"You didn't cry when I left home."

"No, I was glad to see the back of you." She laughed and pulled Alice into her arms. "I cried over you, too. I just didn't let you see it."

"I'm not sure I believe you." She kissed her mother's cheek and bent to look at the kitten in the box. "So, Sugar, are you ready to explore your new home?"

"Where are the keys to the utility truck? Dad said I could use it to move my bed."

"Oh, don't take your bed." Amanda said. "Your room will look so empty."

"God, Mom." Alice took the keys off the hook on the wall. "You sure are making a big deal out of this. She's not moving across the country or anything like that."

"Shut up, Alice." Evelyn elbowed her sister playfully. "I'll bring it back, Mom. I just didn't have the money to buy one after I bought my living room furniture. Keep the door closed until I save up enough money."

"Leave the bed." Jeff came into the room from the garage. "I'll buy you one." He held up a hand when she started to object. "It'll be a housewarming gift from us. I know you want to be independent, but humor us a little."

"That's right." Alice said. "This independence thing can go too far. After all, they bought all of my furniture."

"Yeah." Jeff laughed and hugged both of his daughters. "Sometimes the independence thing doesn't go far enough."

*

"It's lovely!" Amanda said as she and Evelyn struggled to carry the full-sized mattress into the apartment.

"It's kind of small." Jeff and Alice carried the new box spring through the door to the bedroom. "It's a good thing you didn't let me talk you into that queen size bed. It wouldn't have fit into the bedroom."

"It's not that small, Dad." Alice helped him put the mattress on the four-posted frame they had arranged earlier. "My first apartment was an efficiency, remember."

"That didn't last long, though. You upgraded pretty fast."

"Ev will, too. Won't you?"

"Maybe. I don't know. I like this place. It's small, but it just feels right. Sugar likes it, too. I think the two of us will be just fine here for a while."

"Where is Sugar?" Amanda asked.

"Don't tell me you're missing him already." Evelyn laughed

"No, I just don't want him to attack me out of nowhere."

"He's probably asleep behind the drapes in the window seat. Yep." She parted the curtains. "There he is. See, he loves this place." The lazy kitten stretched and yawned showing needle sharp small white teeth.

"You should have named him Dracula." Jeff laughed. "Isn't he cute, Manda? I miss having a cat. Why don't we get one?"

"No more cats, Jeff. You're worse than the kids. I think two dogs, five horses, and a mule are plenty. Not to mention the chickens you brought home for Easter last year."

"Oh, come on. You love Huey, Dewy, and Louie."

"Dad, you do know that those names are for ducks, don't you?" Alice sat down next to the cat on the window seat.

"I guess I was a little confused. What will we name the ducks I bring home next Easter?"

"No ducks, Jeff." Amanda turned to Evelyn. "It's a beautiful apartment, honey. Come on, Jeff, we need to get home to feed the horses."

She left the apartment. Jeff exchanged a worried look with Alice and Evelyn, then left behind her.

*

Evelyn felt like singing the next morning when she went to work. She had walked from her apartment to the nursery. It would have taken her only about ten minutes if she hadn't walked around the duck pond. It was late September in Atlanta and still very warm during the day, but the nights and early mornings were starting to be cool. The fresh air and the brisk walk did wonders to clear her head. It was much better than forty-five minutes in traffic on the highway.

She went through the door and headed to the back of the shop where the employee break room was. Opening her locker, she put her purse into it and smiled. It was nice not having to pack her lunch because she could go home and eat. This was going to be great.

"Hello, sweetheart."

She turned at her dad's voice. "Hey, Dad, you're here early. You usually don't come in until eleven or twelve."

"I told your mom I needed to get in early so she had to feed the horses. I thought maybe she needed to have more to do. With you guys gone, maybe she's feeling like she's not needed anymore. Of course, that isn't true. I need her."

"I know you do. Maybe she's a little worried that you don't need her, though. Remember, Alice snooped through your drawers and found the marriage certificate. We know that either we came very early, or Mom had a very short pregnancy." She laughed.

"Your sister is nosey. You kids never needed to know that."

"Well, we do. Maybe you and Mom should go on a trip or something, a second honeymoon."

"It would actually be a first honeymoon. Mom was too uncomfortable at that point to go anywhere. That's not a bad idea. But who would take care of the animals? Now that you've moved out, I'm sure you wouldn't be able to drive back out there twice a day."

"Get to work planning a trip. Give me a couple of months. I won't mind staying out there for a week or so, once the newness of my apartment wears off."

"I'll suggest it to her. Thanks, honey." He kissed her on the top of the head. "Listen, I want you to work on some plans for a landscaping project. I know I saw some of your assignments at school, but I'd like to see what you can do in real life. I think I have the perfect house for a first project."

"That sounds so nice, Dad, but you'll have to clear it with Darcy."

"I don't have to clear anything with Darcy. I own the place, remember?"

"Dad, please."

"You are the mule of the family. Alice isn't stubborn she's persistent. She got that from me. Your mother is stubborn, and you inherited that."

"I thought Elmo was the mule of the family."

"We have two mules."

"Really, Dad, I need to work things out with Darcy my own way. Even when I take this place over completely, I'll need her. She won't be retiring for another twenty or so years. She knows this place inside and out. I need her."

"Not if she's going to get in your way. You can hire your own manager. Besides, you aren't going to be taking this place over completely for a while. I've got a ways to go."

"I'm glad, but maybe you need to spend a little more time with Mom. I'll handle Darcy. She'll be on my team pretty soon."

"Your team...!" They both turned at the sound of Darcy's voice. There was an uncomfortable minute of silence while they both struggled for the right thing to say.

"That's right," Jeff said. "This is a team. We work together to make this place run."

"It was my understanding that I was the manager and that the person in that position supervised the associates."

"That's right, but it is still a team." Jeff walked to the door and turned before he went through. "Darcy, I have a landscaping job I'd like for Evelyn to design. I'll take her to look at it this afternoon. I made an appointment with the client at 2:00."

"I had plans for her this afternoon. I guess I'll have to have one of the part time boys do it. I really needed them both in the yard. I wish you'd give me more notice."

"I'll remember that." He mouthed 'I'm sorry' to Evelyn before he went through the door.

Great! Evelyn thought. Whatever progress I'd made just went out the window.

Darcy crossed her arms. "I would call that an unfair advantage."

"It was his idea, not mine."

"I'll bet! You'll be on checkout until 2:00." She turned and left the room.

*

The morning dragged, of course. To start with, she really was bad on the checkout line. She lost track of what she'd scanned. If she had to key anything in, she did it wrong and spent too much time correcting it. Customers don't like to wait. She took twice as long as the other cashiers did so the customers were grouchy by the time they got to her. Not only was she bad at it, but she hated it. She would have hated it even if she'd been good at it. The computer screen gave her a headache and her hand ached from holding the scanner.

"It's really nice to see you, Elaine," she said to the person who came to relieve her for lunch.

"Darcy says you can only take half an hour since you're going to be gone all afternoon," the girl said apologetically.

Evelyn closed her eyes for just a second. "Okay, but let me warn you. I'm going to run late getting back. If she gives you a hard time, I'll tell her that you told me but I couldn't help it."

"That's okay. Don't worry about me." The girl took Evelyn's place behind the counter. "I don't know why you take it from her. She doesn't treat the rest of us like that, you know."

"I figured. Otherwise why would you work here. I'll see you in forty-five minutes, tops."

"Take your time."

Evelyn retrieved her purse from the break room and went out the back door to walk around the building and cross the street to her apartment. As she approached the street a car pulled into the parking lot and Helen got out.

"Evelyn!" She called to her and waved.

"Helen." Evelyn went toward the car. "I was just going home to lunch. I live in the apartments over there."

"I'm glad I caught you. I called the number you gave me. Your mother told me you had moved out. I guess I'll need to get your new number."

"Is there something I can do for you?" Evelyn's heart was beating a little more quickly than before. Maybe Helen was going to invite her out to dinner with them and Jamie.

"We're having a party on Saturday night. I wondered if you'd like to come. Jamie will be there. His younger sister Marisa will too. I guess you must know her. She'll be there with her fiancé."

"Oh yes, I babysat for her when she was little. Now that she's grown, we're friends. I'd love to come. Have you mentioned to Jamie that you were going to invite me?"

"No. I'm sure he won't mind though." Helen looked puzzled.

"Oh, I'm sure he wouldn't. Could we let it be a surprise? It'll be fun for both of us."

"Alright. Okay." She smiled. "Well, I wanted to go in and get some top soil. I guess you're going to lunch."

"Yeah, see you Saturday." Evelyn walked to the crosswalk and pressed the button for the light. She glanced over her shoulder and watched Helen go into the nursery. Then she jumped into the air, landing on her feet just as the light turned and the walk signal came on. She hurried across the street with a smile on her face.

*

"I'm back, Elaine." Evelyn stood to the side of the checkout counter. "Have there been any fireworks?"

"Oh yes," Elaine said. She didn't look stressed in any way, though.

"I hope I didn't get you into any trouble."

Elaine finished checking out the customer in front of her then reached under the counter for her water bottle. "No, no."

She smiled. "When she asked me about it, I threw you right under the bus."

"Good!" Evelyn laughed. "That's exactly what I wanted you to do."

As Elaine left the shop Darcy walked in. She stalked to the counter and looked directly at Evelyn without saying a word.

"Did you want something, Darcy?"

"I told Elaine to tell you to be back in half an hour. It's been fifty minutes."

"It takes ten minutes for me to get to my apartment and ten minutes back. Ten minutes is just not enough time to eat lunch."

"You should have eaten in the break room."

"I didn't bring my lunch because I always get an hour. I didn't think I needed to. Did you just want me to go hungry? I don't eat much breakfast. If I don't eat lunch I get light headed by dinner time."

"There is a café upstairs."

"It's the lunch rush. It would have taken me longer up there."

Darcy just looked at her. After a minute, a customer approached the counter. Evelyn greeted her and started checking her out. Darcy pushed herself away from the counter and left the room. It was starting to look like standing her ground was going to be the only way to get things worked out between the two of them. That wasn't ideal, but maybe that was the way it had to be.

"All set?" Jeff asked as he approached the counter an hour later.

"All set." Evelyn turned to the other cashier. "Do you think you can handle it by yourself until the afternoon shift gets here?"

"No problem."

"Jeff, Ev," Darcy called as they started for the door. They turned. She approached them with a smiling middle-aged woman following her. "Before you leave I'd like you to meet Lindsey Delmer. She's going to be our new cashier."

It was the first time Evelyn had seen Darcy smile since she'd started working at the nursery. "It's nice to meet you, Lindsey." She extended her hand to her.

"Lindsey," Darcy said. "This is Jeff Landrum, the owner of Landrum's, and his daughter, Evelyn."

"It's so nice to meet you. I hope I'll fit in here. I'm really excited about the job. I love to garden."

"Then you will definitely fit in," Jeff said as he shook her hand. "We have an appointment we have to get to, or we'd stay and help you get settled in."

Evelyn smiled at her dad. She knew he wasn't just being gracious. He meant it. He really would have stayed to help the new employee get settled in.

"Well, thank you. I'm sure I'll do fine. You go ahead."

They left the building and got into the company truck. "She seems nice." Evelyn said.

"I told Darcy I didn't want you on checkout anymore." He held up his hand as she started to object. "I know you don't want me to interfere, but you've done your time there. You know what you'll be asking your employees to do. You hate it, don't you?"

"Yes, but Dad ..."

He held up his hand again. "Evelyn, you're screwing up the books."

"Oh." She sighed and looked out the window. "So that's why Darcy looked so happy."

*

"Oh, Dad!" Evelyn stepped out of the truck onto the muddy front yard of a newly built home. "It's beautiful. The potential here is fantastic."

"You are definitely my daughter. I looked at this place and saw the same thing you do. However, I think we may be very much alone." He looked around at the property. It was a lot that backed up to one of the major interstate highways that ran through Atlanta. The highway was probably about a hundred feet above it, so the sound wasn't too much of a problem, but the house was built up against the hill that ran up to the road. There was a small front yard that would be easy enough, but in the back of the house there was a patch of ground about ten feet by twenty, then a solid wall of rock up to the highway.

Evelyn walked into the middle of the muddy front yard. She looked up at the sky then took a compass out of her pocket and looked at it. "Okay, we're facing pretty much due south. This yard will do great with full sun plants. The back, of course, with the hill will be divided. The part shaded by the house, the part down low, will do better with shade plants. But that hill, Dad." She looked at him and his eyes reflected her enthusiasm. "The hill is a blank canvas. It will get strong sun in some places. That will be great for sun worshiping vines like jasmine and cypress vine. The shady parts could house air feeders. How much are these people willing to pay?"

He smiled and put his arm across her shoulder. "They do have a budget, but it isn't too limited. I want you to get the feel of the place. Do what you need to do to figure out what will grow where. Then we'll talk about the budget and what we can afford when we get back to the shop."

"Okay." She looked around. This was what she'd spent five years in school to do. This was what she'd dreamed of doing all of her life. She took a deep breath, steadied her heartbeat, and started around the side of the house. She'd walk the whole lot, get the feel of the place.

Chapter 4

"I'm so nervous. What if he snubs me?" Evelyn turned to look at the back of her dress in the mirror. She was dressing for the party. Alice was there to help her and to provide moral support.

"Now come on, Ev. We've known Jamie all our lives. Do you honestly think he's ever snubbed anyone? He's probably more worried that you'll snub him."

"He can't be. He doesn't know I'm coming. I asked Helen not to tell him."

"Why in the world?"

"I was afraid he wouldn't come if he knew I would be there."

"Ev, you're so insecure."

"He's avoided me like the plague, Al. I just think he would have stayed away if he knew I was coming. Which, in a way, is encouraging. He must still have feelings for me if he's trying to stay away from me. I just hope they aren't bad feelings, because I'm not giving up until I have an answer that satisfies me, one way or the other."

"You mean until you get a yes answer. I don't think a no answer is ever going to satisfy you."

"No, I don't think so either." She brushed her hair and turned to her sister. "Well, how do I look?"

"You look gorgeous. That dress is perfect on you. Which means it would be perfect on me. Too bad I didn't see it first."

"Wish me luck." Evelyn picked up her purse and opened the door. "Oh!" She jumped back startled. Marisa and a very attractive young man stood on the doorstep.

"Marisa, you startled me." She laughed.

"I'm sorry I was just about to knock. On the way to the party it dawned on me that you might like to come with us. That way you don't have to walk into a room full of people you don't know all by yourself."

"Thanks for thinking of me. I'd love to go in with you, but I'll take my own car in case I need to leave early." She turned to the young man. "You must be Mike."

"Yes I am."

"I'm sorry," Marisa said. "I should have introduced you. Oh, and this is Evelyn's sister Alice."

"I don't suppose the two of you are twins?" Mike laughed.

"No, no, and you can hardly tell we're sisters." They all laughed.

"Shall we go?" Evelyn said.

"I'm sure it would be alright for you to come to the party with us, Alice. The more the merrier."

"Thanks, but, I always work the dinner shift on Saturday. I'll be a little late today, but that's okay. I'm the owner." She pulled the door closed behind her and Evelyn locked it. "Have a good time, Ev." She kissed her sister's cheek and turned to walk to her apartment across the complex.

"You aren't too nervous are you, Evelyn?"

"Why would she be nervous?" Mike asked.

"Don't be insensitive." She elbowed him playfully in the belly.

"Okay, well let's go then. You can follow us, Evelyn."

Twenty minutes later Evelyn entered a charming renovated older house in the mid-town area of Atlanta. It was an older neighborhood with the more typical southern homes. They had large front porches. This one had a porch swing. Evelyn had always wanted a porch swing. She was charmed by the place.

The feeling stopped abruptly when she entered the living room to see Jamie across the room talking to a very pretty blond and leaning a little too close to her. Her heart started to pound.

"Maybe I shouldn't have come."

"I don't know who she is, but I really don't think he's seeing anyone." Marisa whispered.

"What are you two talking about?" Mike asked from behind them.

"Nothing." At that moment Jamie looked up and his eyes met Evelyn's. At first his face registered surprise then a kind of weary look came over him and his shoulders visibly slumped.

"Oh, man," Evelyn said. "He really doesn't want to see me."

Mike must not have heard her because at that moment he raised his hand and called across the crowded room. "Hey, Jamie."

Evelyn wished the ground would open up and suck her in. Just as she was contemplating turning and quietly leaving the party, Helen approached.

"You made it. I'm so glad. I was afraid you'd gotten lost."

"No, Marisa and Mike came by my apartment. I followed them here."

"Good, come on. Let me introduce you to my husband and our friends." Helen took Evelyn's hand and pulled her across the room to the refreshment table. Jamie was only a few feet away from her. The girl had moved off and was talking to a group of people.

"Of course, you know Jamie," she said. "And this is my husband Don."

Evelyn was surprised at Don. He was probably a head shorter than Helen, and though he was pleasant looking, he wore a loose pair of trousers supported by suspenders. The trousers were hiked up under his arms. His hair looked like he had just gotten out of bed, and his glasses frames were so big they made his head look small.

Helen was so tall and beautiful and well put together. What an interesting pair.

"It's nice to meet you, Evelyn. It's nice to meet the owner of the store my wife spends all her money in."

"Not all of my money, and besides, it's our money." Helen laughed.

"It's nice to meet you, too. Hello, Jamie.

"Hey, Evelyn. I see the scratches on your nose have healed without a scar."

"They were very superficial."

"How's the little demon doing? How are the ferals?"

"They're settling in really well. Did you name them? We're calling them Sterling and Red. Naming our animals after colors seems to be a theme at our house these days."

"I called them Orange and Silver. So that fits. What about the little guy?"

"Sugar."

He laughed. Evelyn smiled at him. She loved his laugh. It was musical.

"Sugar does not fit that little devil. But he's your cat." He looked at her for a minute, his face still lit up in a genuine smile. Then he shook his head a little. "It was good seeing you, Evelyn. I see a friend across the room. I should go greet her." He was gone before she could say anything.

"That was rude." Helen stepped into the place Jamie had just left. "I've never seen Jamie act like that." She looked at Evelyn's face and winced. She must have read her feelings in her expression. "What's going on between you two? I think it's time you talked to me about it. I'd like it if we could become friends."

Evelyn had followed Jamie across the room with her eyes. She looked back at Helen. She couldn't trust herself to talk. Her throat was swollen with a huge lump. She could feel her eyes swimming.

"I'm sorry." Marisa put a hand on her arm. Evelyn looked down at the floor.

"I guess I shouldn't have come."

"Of course, you should have come. It's my party and I wanted you here," Helen said. "Why don't you get yourself a glass of wine and come outside on the deck with me. We can talk out there. I'd like to show you my garden anyway."

"I'll come along." Marisa poured them all three a glass of wine and Evelyn let herself be led through the back door to the yard.

"I can't talk right now." Evelyn's voice was unsteady.

"We'll walk around the garden first." Helen linked their arms. "It's dark, but I have it lit pretty well. I think you'll be able to see."

The garden was beautiful. Helen described the planning of it and some of the plants. She asked questions about the plants that she couldn't remember names of. She asked some questions about the care and cultivation of them. Evelyn felt herself relax as her interest in the subject was piqued. The lump in her throat melted away and her eyes dried up.

"Evelyn," Helen said. "You don't have to talk to me about Jamie. But it might help. I can tell you that he isn't really very happy. I mean, he loves his work. He loves his volunteer work with the animals. But something is missing. I've worried about it for years. Don says it's none of my business. He says I should keep out of it. But Jamie is such a nice person."

They had stopped at a swing on the far end of the yard well away from the group of people that was gathering on the porch. They all sat down on the swing in a row.

Evelyn laughed. "Are you sure this thing can hold us all?"

"It's held Marisa and me many times. You can't add much weight. You're tiny."

They all sat in silence for a minute.

"Jamie and I were in love when I went away to school." Evelyn started in a whisper. "I don't know what happened. He says he doesn't love me anymore. I'm trying not to believe that, but I'm becoming more and more convinced."

Marisa sighed. "Evelyn, I don't know what's going on with him. I think Mom knows but she isn't saying anything, not even to Dad. He's moody. He won't tell us where he lives. Now that's just plain weird. I see a lot of him at the school when I'm visiting Mike. He's nice and all, but something just isn't right."

"That's right." Helen pushed the swing backwards from the ground and they all put their feet in the air. "He won't tell us where he lives either. We used to go to his apartment for dinner and the golf tournament every year. We did it at our house this year. I don't think it's you he doesn't love anymore. I think it's something about himself."

"Ev, don't give up, at least until you get an explanation. He hasn't given you one, has he?"

"No. He just says it's over."

"Has he actually said he doesn't love you anymore?"

"He says he'll always love me because he's known me so long, but only as a friend."

"I hate it when people say that," Marisa said. "It's such a cop out."

"No one's ever said it to me before. I guess I've never cared enough about anybody else. But I didn't like it either. Listen," she stood up. "I think I'll just go on home. I'm really not in the mood to go in and make polite conversation right now.

Thanks for inviting me, Helen. I'm sorry to take you away from your guests."

She walked to the house. She wished she could just skirt around the house to her car, but she'd left her purse inside. She put her wineglass on the kitchen counter and turned to leave. Her face collided with Jamie's chest as she turned. She stayed that way for a second remembering the scent of him. His hands came to her arms and she looked up at his face. He looked like he felt guilty. That was not the emotion she was hoping for.

"Look, Evelyn. I'm sorry I was rude. I didn't expect to see you here tonight. I wish Helen had told me you were coming."

"I asked her not to."

"Why?"

"Would you have come if you knew?"

He stepped back and let go of her arms. "I don't know."

"See why? Now, if you'll just step aside, I'll go home. Then you can enjoy your friends without my unwanted company." She pushed past him and went out the door.

*

She stacked paving stones at work on Monday morning. For once, she was glad for the list of store room jobs that Darcy had handed her when she got in. She didn't want to see anyone. She didn't want to talk to anyone. She didn't want to think about anything. The work wasn't helping with the thinking. Her mind just wouldn't stop, but the physical labor was working off some of the pain and frustration.

Her mind was going over and over the events of the past five years. When had Jamie started to pull away from her? It was not long after she'd gone to school. What could possibly have happened?

"What are you doing?" Alice asked. Evelyn turned to look at her. Alice stood in the doorway of the stock room with her arms crossed. The familiar expression of disdain made Evelyn laugh. The laughter seemed to relieve some of the tension she'd felt all morning. She straightened for the first time noticing the stiffness in her back and sat down on the loading cart.

"I'm stacking paving stones."

"I can't believe you let her make you do that. That's not a job for a woman of your size."

"I don't know what it has to do with size. I'm getting really sick of hearing about my size. You don't have to be big to be strong," she snapped as her mood went from the briefly felt lightness back to brooding.

"I guess not." Alice dropped her arms to her sides. "I didn't mean to make you mad, Ev. What happened at the party on Saturday? Judging from your present mood, it didn't go too well."

"I don't want to talk about it."

"I figured you didn't since I couldn't find you all day yesterday. I called and went to your apartment. Dad said you took Roan out all by yourself. He said you'd gone before he had time to stop you. You know he doesn't like for us to ride alone and he's right. What if you fell off and got hurt."

"I'm an excellent rider. Besides, I stayed to the path along the road. If I'd gotten hurt someone would have seen me. I'm not suicidal, Alice." She turned and grabbed another stone to heave onto the top of the pile. "Ouch," she said and pressed her fingers to the scratch she had just made on the side of her arm.

"I'm not so sure." Alice walked to her and pulled her into a hug.

"Don't be nice to me. I'll cry."

"Maybe you should."

"I don't want to." She pulled away and brushed at the tears that threatened to spill onto her cheeks.

"You've wiped dirt all over your face." Alice walked to the sink and wet a cloth. She cleaned the smudges from Evelyn's cheeks. "Talk to me."

"Why does everyone think talking will help? In fact, I don't think anything will help. I'm going to give up, Al. I need to get on with my life. And if that life doesn't include Jamie, I'd better get used to it."

"I don't like to hear you talk like that. I was counting on having Jamie as my brother-in-law. I can't believe there's anyone else out there I wouldn't mind sharing you with."

"There isn't anyone out there for me at all. I'll just go it alone." She walked to the sink, took off her gloves, threw them a little too forcefully into the laundry box, and dipped her hands under the faucet she had just turned on. "Ouch," she said. The water was too hot.

Alice tapped her chin with her finger. "I think it's time I got involved."

Evelyn whirled around. "Oh no, you don't! All I need is you mixed up in this. Besides, like I said, there isn't anything for you to get involved in. I'm quitting. I'll mend my broken heart and get on with my work. Now if you will excuse me I need to go out to the site I'm designing. Did I tell you Dad gave me a design project? I'm so excited." She forced a smile that she hoped looked enthusiastic.

Alice slanted her eyes at her then straightened her expression. "Okay," she said. "I guess you're right. I'll stay out of it."

"Uh oh," Evelyn said under her breath as she watched her sister leave the room.

She went to her locker to get her purse and keys. She picked up a notebook and some sketching pencils she'd brought. She tiptoed out the break room door and past the office. Her dad hadn't come in that day, so Darcy was in high form. She was a little more subdued with her supervision when she thought Jeff might walk in on her, but when he wasn't there she became a tyrant.

"Where do you think you're going?" Darcy said from behind her.

Shoot, she thought. She was past the office and she thought she'd gotten away.

She turned around. "I'm going out to the site to get a look at the noon sun. I need to see every time of the day to start designing the landscape."

"You were just going to go without asking my permission?"

"I figured you'd find something else for me to do so I couldn't leave. What's the problem, Darcy? You seem to be in my way no matter what I do. Just what is your problem?"

"I beg your pardon!" Darcy fisted her hands by her sides. "Don't you talk to me like that, young lady. I am still your supervisor."

"You know what, Darcy!" Evelyn squared her shoulders and looked right into Darcy's eyes. "No, you are not! Dad said I would learn the business from the bottom up. I don't remember him saying anything about you being my supervisor."

"He asked me to guide you through all the procedures. That's supervision."

"Well he didn't say anything about me spending the rest of my life in the storage room or on the loading dock. Now if you will excuse me I have work to do." She turned to leave.

"You come back here. You will not sneak out of here without my permission."

Evelyn turned around again slowly. She looked back at Darcy. "You're right," she said calmly. "I will not sneak out of here. I won't sneak out of here ever again. I will inform you of my plans because that is the courteous thing to do. Did you get that? I will inform you. I will not ask your permission." She turned again and walked through the door.

"Bravo!" Alice stood on the other side of the door. "You finally got up the nerve to put her in her place."

"Shut up, Alice." Evelyn looked in her sister's direction long enough to trip over a wagon that was in her way. She caught herself on a plant stand but dropped everything in her hands. She gathered her purse, keys, and notepad and stormed to her car.

*

The tears had not fallen. She'd managed to dry them up before they overflowed her lower eye lids. She sat on a rock that jutted out of the high wall of rock and dirt in the back yard of the house. It was going to be a challenge to make something of this yard. The wall was spectacular really, and since sound tends to go up you could hardly hear the highway. She looked up at the guard rail at the top of the hill.

"Just the same," she said out loud to herself. "I don't think I'd want to live here. What if a car came crashing through that guard rail?"

"We've thought of that." She looked up, startled. "A woman stood at the back door of the house. She was young, maybe thirty and very pretty. Her hair was brown and her eyes were the same color. She reminded Evelyn of her mother.

"We're going to build a barrier on this side of the guard rail. We had to petition to be able to do it, but they finally said yes." She held out her hand to Evelyn. "I'm Ruth Martin. I gather you're Evelyn, Mr. Landrum's daughter. He told us you would be working on the design of our landscape."

Evelyn slipped off the ledge in the cliff. She brushed off her hands on her jeans and shook the proffered hand. "It's nice to meet you. I didn't realize anyone would be here today. I didn't think you'd moved in yet."

"We haven't," she said. "I'm just getting ideas for the interior of the house. It's our first house and I can't wait to start decorating it."

"I guess that is pretty exciting. Do you garden at all? Do you have anything you would particularly want in the yard?"

"No, no, Adam is the gardener. He doesn't do much actually, but he's the one that enjoys the yard. He'll putter, but we'll pay someone to do most of the work."

"Does he have any ideas?"

"Yes, he isn't here right now, but I think we have a meeting with you on Wednesday. Is that the right day? I think Mr. Landrum said 10:00 am."

"Hmm … he must have forgotten to tell me."

"Oh dear, is that alright? We can reschedule if you want."

"No, 10:00 o'clock Wednesday is fine with me." She looked at the rocky wall behind them. "I have some great ideas for this hill. I can't wait to run them by you."

"Good. Would you like to come in and have some iced tea? I have a big jug of it."

"No thanks, I'll just wander around out here. I just need to figure out where the sun hits at what time of day, how much the hill shades the yard, that kind of thing."

"Well, if you'll excuse me then, I'll go inside and figure out similar things in there."

"Sure, great, it was nice to meet you." Evelyn felt a little uncomfortable knowing someone was in the house, but as the afternoon wore on and she sketched in her notebook she forgot all about it.

This was what she'd dreamed of. She knew it was important to learn it all. She agreed that happy employees were important, and employees were always happier with an employer who was willing to work right beside them if the need should arise. She felt a little bad about confronting Darcy the way she had. She smiled. No, she didn't. It needed to be done. She was finished being a wimp. She'd get what she wanted in her work even if she didn't get what she wanted with Jamie.

"Evelyn." She looked up to see Ruth crossing the small yard toward her. "I'm going to leave now before the traffic gets too bad, but come and have some tea and cookies with me first."

Evelyn looked at her watch. "It's already 4:00 in the afternoon. Gosh, where did the time go?" She put her pencils in her purse and went over to the little folding table that Ruth was setting up. She picked up one of the folding chairs and put it beside the table.

"It's shady here in the afternoon," Ruth said. "Adam and I love to sit outside in the late afternoon before dinner. Maybe we could put a little patio right here."

"I think that would be very nice. Of course, it's early fall now. The sun will be lower in the sky in the winter so it will be shadier here. In the summer, it should be right overhead and that'll be hot. Maybe a covered porch would be nice."

"Or an awning, I've seen some awnings that look nice."

"I'll gather some brochures for you to look over."

"Sounds good."

"How did the interior decorating go? Is that a hobby, or do you do it for a living?"

"I actually studied it in school. Most people don't bother with that. It isn't necessary to have credentials in interior decorating."

"It isn't in landscaping either, but I went to school, too. I just wanted to have that to back me up. Have you worked in the field?"

"No, we have a son. A lot of people wouldn't think that was a lot of work, but ours has been a challenge. I've been pretty busy with that."

"Is he special in some way?" She didn't want to pry, but Ruth wouldn't have brought it up if she minded her asking.

"He's special in just about every way." She laughed. "He's a genius. I know all mothers think that, but his IQ is astonishingly high. You know being smarter than everyone can be as big a handicap as anything."

"I guess so."

"He's also more athletic. My concern is that he'll be able to scale that wall at only four years old."

"Maybe this isn't the best location for you." Evelyn looked at the steep hill to the highway.

"We thought about that, but we discussed it with Bradley and he convinced us that he was not going to do anything that stupid." She laughed and looked at her watch. "I've got to go. Adam came home a little early today to stay with Bradley when he got home from his play group. He's home schooled. We just couldn't find a school that could accommodate him. But he has a home school group so that he gets some socialization. Adam will be pacing the floor looking at his watch at this point." She laughed and stood to fold the table and gather her things.

"It was great to meet you, Ruth," Evelyn said as she carried one of the chairs and the bag Ruth had put the tea and cookies in to Ruth's car. "I guess I'll see you Wednesday."

"That's right, Wednesday. I'll see you then."

Ruth got into her car and backed out of the driveway. Evelyn stood beside her own car and watched her drive away. For the first time since she'd come home she felt strong. She was really into the business now. This was her future, the future she'd worked toward all of her life. She sighed, sad that Jamie wouldn't be sharing it with her. But at least she had this.

*

The phone was ringing as she entered her apartment. She hurried to look at the caller ID. It was Jeff.

"Hey, Dad."

"I ... Uh ... it's going to take me a while to get used to this caller ID thing. I'm not used to people knowing who I am before I say hello."

"You'll get used to it." She laughed.

"You sound happy. Did good things happen today?"

"Some good things, I guess it depends on who you are as to the other things." She thought of her show down with Darcy.

"Is that a riddle?"

"No. So what's up?"

"Honey, Darcy called me at home this afternoon."

"Uh oh."

"I'm not mad at you. I just think we need to talk about things. For one thing, I'm sure Darcy is exaggerating. I'm sure you wouldn't have said all those terrible things to her."

"What terrible things?"

"I want to talk about it tomorrow at the nursery. I think the three of us should get together and work this out. Darcy's been a God send to me for more than twenty years. She's important. But you're my daughter. You'll take my place someday."

"You're not going anywhere, Dad."

He laughed. "Not anytime soon, but someday. That brings up the other thing I need to talk to you about. Honey, I'm really worried about your mother. She's not herself. Yesterday she didn't even come out of her workshop until bed time. I couldn't coax her out for lunch or dinner."

"Well, that's not a bad thing. You know she loves to make her soap and those paintings that she downloads the stencils for from the internet. Maybe she's snapping out of this thing and getting interested again."

"That's what I was thinking, but I knocked on the door about midafternoon. She told me to come in. She was just sitting in front of the window looking out."

"You don't think she was taking a break?"

"None of her equipment or paints were disturbed. It looks like she hasn't done anything with them in months. I'm worried. I don't know what to do."

"Maybe you should take her to a doctor."

"I've suggested it, but she won't go. I'm afraid to leave her, Ev. I need to come in tomorrow to deal with this thing with you and Darcy, but I'm afraid to leave her alone. Alice said she'd drop by about mid-morning. She's going to try to get her to go to the barn with her. She thought a little time with Sterling and Red would help. I doubt she'll have any luck. I haven't been able to get her to go."

"Gosh, Dad. I don't know what to do either."

"I was hoping you girls would come to dinner this weekend. I know you're both off on Sunday. How about come early, take the horses out in the ring. Maybe she'll come out to see them. I've talked to Alice. She'll be here."

"Great, I'll be there, too."

"I've got a couple of people coming out to look at Roan and Dapple. I'm having a little trouble finding them homes since I'd like to keep them together. I'm hopeful this time. They'll be here at 2:00. Come after that."

"Please don't sell Roan and Dapple, Dad."

There was only silence on the line.

"Dad, please don't sell them."

"Honey, I didn't realize you were getting so attached."

"Well, I am. Please don't sell them." She hadn't realized it herself until just now.

"Honey, you can't keep them in your apartment." He laughed, but he sounded uneasy.

"Please..."

"We'll talk about it this weekend."

"Don't sell them before then."

"I won't. I promise."

*

The next morning she went to work earlier than usual. She hadn't slept well worrying about her meeting with Jeff and Darcy. What had Darcy claimed she'd said? She'd gone over everything in her head. She couldn't remember saying anything terrible to her. Unless being assertive was terrible. However, she hoped Jeff wouldn't confront her with it. It wouldn't help the already difficult relationship she had with Darcy.

She had finally fallen asleep around 2:00 am. But she didn't sleep as late as usual. She was just too wound up.

"Hey, Dad." She stood in the doorway to his office.

"Good morning, sweetie." He got up and came around the desk to give her a bear hug. "Come in here I want to show you something." He guided her across the hall of the business suite. There were three offices in the suite. His, of course, and Darcy's, and there was an empty one that had belonged to his former partner.

He opened the door to the empty one and guided her in.

"Dad, don't tell me you're going to give me an office."

"Why not? That's exactly what I'm going to do."

"This isn't going to help with Darcy."

"Honey, I'm sure Darcy will recognize the need for you to have your own work space. That's what it is really. It's a workspace. I plan to give a lot of the landscaping plans to you now. It's time I took a little more time at home. I think that's part of your mom's trouble. She's there all alone too much. Besides, I want to spend more time with her. I thought we'd travel a little, see some of the world."

"I think that's great, Dad. Really, I appreciate you wanting me to have a work space but I do fine in the break room."

"No, I want you in here." He walked around the room. He put a hand on the drafting table in front of the window. "This furniture was Victoria's. You can change it all if you want to. Just tell me what you want and I'll pay for it."

She went to the center of the room and turned around assessing the furniture.

"If you think you'd work better on a flat surface we can replace the drafting table with something that would suit you better."

"No, I like to work on a drafting table. I'd like to have one in my apartment, but there isn't room. I've been using the dining room table."

"If you had a work space here, you could do most of your work here. I know you'll take some of it home with you. You're a chip off the old block." He laughed.

Evelyn smiled and looked around at the other furniture. There was a wire cabinet with drawers for equipment. She could use that, but the desk was bulky and only had three drawers.

"I'd like to replace the desk and get a chair, a nice chair that's comfortable to sit in."

"You do the shopping and tell me the cost. Maybe you could go out for a little while this afternoon. The sooner you're in here doing the work, the sooner I can spend more time at home."

"You're really worried, aren't you? I've never seen you want to spend less time here. This place has always been your life."

"This place was my life for a long time. But since your mom came into it, she's been my life. Not that I don't still love my work. I'll always keep a hand in it, but right now I want to be at home with her."

"Oh, Dad," There was a lump in her throat. She put her arms around him and buried her face in his chest. He stroked her back. She knew he had sensed her need to collect herself because he didn't say anything for a few minutes.

"It'll be alright, Ev. We'll work it out."

"I was just thinking it's a shame every woman can't find a man like you."

"I have my faults." He laughed and stepped away to look at her. "I take it young James isn't responding the way you'd like him to."

"He isn't responding at all. I've decided to give up and move on with my life. He doesn't have to see me if he doesn't want to. I can't force it."

"Honey ..."

"I'd rather not talk about it."

"Good morning." Evelyn heaved a sigh of relief as Darcy interrupted them. She stood in the doorway of the room. There was a smile on her face, but a different expression in her eyes. The smile, Evelyn knew, was for her dad. The expression in her eyes, whatever it was, was for her.

"Good morning, Darcy," Jeff said. "Let's all go into my office and have a talk, shall we?"

"Alright." Darcy stepped aside and motioned for them to pass. Evelyn went through the door and Jeff waited for Darcy to follow her. They went into his office and he sat down behind the desk while Darcy and Evelyn sat in chairs across from him.

Evelyn smiled a little nervously. He always had a way of taking control of a situation but she wasn't sure this was going to work in her favor. And how would he approach their little face off of the previous day. Confrontation was very uncomfortable for her. She'd had enough for a while.

"Darcy," he said. "I really appreciate the help you're giving Evelyn. I know firsthand that even when you've studied a subject as extensively as she has, the real experience can be very different."

Start with praise. Evelyn remembered her business administration courses in school.

"I know that I said that Evelyn should start from the bottom up, and she agreed with that."

"I've tried to introduce her to all aspects of the behind the scenes associates," Darcy said. "She needs to know what they do in order to inspire them to do it."

"Exactly," Jeff continued. "And we've tried the checkout line. She's learned what they do. And we've learned that we don't want her to do that anymore." He smiled knowingly at Darcy. They both laughed.

"No, we don't." Darcy flashed Evelyn a smile that was more like a smirk.

Evelyn smiled back. Okay, she thought, start with praise but it isn't necessary to humiliate me. She stretched the smile a little wider.

"I think it's time for Evelyn to move up, though. I'd like to see her work in the greenhouses and the growing yard when she isn't designing landscape."

Evelyn felt rather than saw Darcy stiffen and sit up a little straighter.

"I'm not sure she's ready for that. I don't think she's ready for the landscaping either."

"No," Jeff said, and Evelyn felt herself getting angry. "She probably isn't. We're never really ready for something new. I know you will help her with anything you can. I know I can count on you for that."

"Of course."

"I'll help her with the landscaping part. I know you haven't done that part since you got out of school."

"You always wanted that for yourself." Darcy was sounding like a petulant child at this point.

"Yes, I did." He smiled and dropped the subject. "I'm going to fix Victoria's old office up as a work room for Ev. She needs a space to spread out her plans."

"She was doing okay in the break room. I was going to use that room for storage."

"We'll find another space for storage."

"Alright." Darcy moved forward in her chair indicating that she was ready to leave.

"Good. Shall we start the day?"

"Yes." Evelyn stood to leave. She hadn't said a word during the whole meeting.

"Ev?" Jeff stopped her. "You've been quiet. Is there anything you wanted to say?"

"No, Sir."

"Sir, that's a new one." Jeff stood up signaling the end of the meeting. "I'd like you to work in the growing yard today. We're getting into fall now. The soil needs turning and sifting. We'll be planting for winter crops in a few more weeks."

Evelyn laughed. He'd been called a glorified farmer by his family. He sure talked like one.

"Okay," she said. "I'll go put up my things and get started."

*

She pulled into the driveway of her parent's home, well, her home. It would always be her home. Alice was already there. The gate was open and she could see the pink Porsche sitting in front of the house. She started down the drive, stopped at the gate to the rescue barn, and got out of the car. Roan was standing at the fence. She swished her tail and whinnied.

"Hey, girl." Evelyn got out of the car and started toward the horse. "Woah!" She stopped and hurried back to the car to check the gears and parking break. Everything was okay so she started back to the waiting horse. Dapple had joined Roan at the fence. She greeted them both.

"Hey, guys. You okay?" She stroked the soft muzzles one at a time. "I hope you weren't too nice to the people who came to look at you. I don't want you to go. I love you guys." Both horses nuzzled her neck. She turned toward her car and continued toward the house.

"Anybody home?" She called as she went through the kitchen door. There was no response. She listened at the bottom of the steps and heard nothing. She walked through the house listening to get an idea of where to look. She didn't hear a sound. There was a door to the back yard off the hallway. She looked out the window and there they were. The three of them were sitting at the table beside the pool drinking something that looked like lemonade. Evelyn smiled. Her dad loved lemonade. Maybe her mom wasn't feeling too bad anymore if she'd made him some.

"Hey, guys." She hurried around the pool to join them. "I guess you started without me." She sat down and poured herself a glass from the pitcher.

"I've only been here for a few minutes." Alice lifted her glass. It was almost full. "Dad was just telling me about your meeting with Darcy."

"There's nothing much to tell." Evelyn gave Jeff what she hoped was a meaningful look.

"I don't know. It sounds to me like Dad did a pretty good job of putting her in her place."

"I don't think it was a matter of …"

"Don't get defensive." Alice held up her hand. "I'm just glad you get to do some of the things you like to do now."

"Me too." Evelyn relaxed and sipped her lemonade. "That reminds me, Dad, I met with Adam and Ruth Martin on Wednesday. I was surprised you didn't want to be there. It was my first meeting with a real client. I thought you'd want to observe."

"I didn't need to. I knew you'd do a good job. So how did it go?"

"I think it went well. I liked them both and I think they liked me."

"That's good, but you know you won't like all of your clients. You'll have to work with them anyway."

"I know, but I'm glad that I like my first ones. It'll be challenge enough doing my first job. I'd like to wait for the challenge of working with difficult clients."

"I don't blame you." Jeff poured himself another glass of lemonade.

"Don't drink too much of it, Jeff," Amanda said. Evelyn realized her mother hadn't spoken until then. She hadn't even said hello. "You know it makes your stomach burn if you drink too much."

"Yes, dear." Jeff smiled and reached across the table to squeeze her hand.

She smiled back, pushed her chair out and dropped his hand. "I think I'll go and mix up the potato salad. I'm sure the potatoes are chilled by now." She turned and walked toward the house. All three of them watched her until the door was closed.

"Things aren't any better, are they?" Alice asked.

"I'm scared to death." Jeff rubbed his eyes with both hands.

"I thought maybe she felt better since she made lemonade," Evelyn said.

"I made it. She told me how. That was the most I could get out of her."

"It's scary, Dad." Alice pulled his hand away from his face.

"Have you talked anymore about going to the doctor?"

"She freezes up when I bring it up. I don't know what to do. I brought her flowers the other day. She said she hated cut flowers. They were so much prettier in the garden still alive."

"I'm sorry, Dad." Evelyn took his other hand. "I think I'll go in and talk to her about the horses. By the way, I really want to keep them. I want them both."

"Ev," Jeff said. "We try not to get attached to the foster horses we take in. If they can be placed in a good home it leaves room for older or sick horses that can't be placed. There's room in Doris's barn, but you know she won't accept anyone but Elmo."

"Dad, I'll find another place to board them when I start making more money. I'll take a bigger salary when I start to bring in more business. Which reminds me, I'd like to talk to you about an idea I have. Not right now, though, I'm going in and talking Mom into going to the barn with me.

"Maybe we should all go." Alice started to stand.

"No, that looks like a set up. I'll go first with her. Then you two can join us."

"And that's not a set up." Jeff laughed.

"It is, but it's not an obvious one."

Evelyn got up and went into the house. Her mom was just sliding the potato salad into the refrigerator. She washed her hands and dried them on her apron. Evelyn walked up behind her and untied the apron strings.

"What are you doing?" Amanda turned around and smiled sadly.

"Come out to the stables with me, Mom. I want to go and visit the cats and I want to see Roan and Dapple. I'm hoping I can enlist your help in talking Dad into keeping them."

"I don't know what I can do. The rescue work is his project."

"It used to be your project, too. Have you even gone down to see Doris lately? She's your horse."

"She's really more your dad's horse now."

"Come on, Mom. Please."

Looking resigned, Amanda put the apron on a hook under the counter and followed Evelyn out the kitchen door.

"Look, Mom. There's Sterling." She pointed at the cat peeking around the door to Doris's barn. "Red won't be far behind. The rat situation has greatly improved since they came." She opened the gate and nudged her mother through it.

Doris was grazing in the far corner of the field with Elmo right next to her. When the gate opened she picked up her head to look. When she saw Amanda, her ears perked up and she started toward them at a limping trot.

"She's just getting more and more lame." Amanda turned around. "I can't stand to see it."

"Look how happy she is to see you, Mom. Even Elmo is coming to see you." Evelyn put a hand on her arm to stop her from going back out the gate.

The horse and the mule stopped a few feet from them. Doris bobbed her head and moved toward Amanda. She nudged her arm with her muzzle.

"She wants you to pet her, Mom. Go ahead. You'll hurt her feelings if you don't."

Amanda stroked the horse's soft neck and leaned her head against it. Her eyes filled with tears and Evelyn stepped back. Her own eyes filled with tears. She didn't know what to do. Mom never cried.

"Look, Mom. Here come Sterling and Red. They're really nice cats, a little skittish. I guess that's to be expected of ferals. But once they get to know you they'll let you pick them up." She scooped Red up and put him quickly into her mother's arms. She didn't give her a chance to object. The cat was startled at first then settled down and started to purr.

Evelyn picked up Silver and held her close to the other cat. "I hate to say it, but they're definitely nicer than Sugar. I love him, but he's really bad."

"He hasn't hurt you again, has he?" Amanda put the cat down and walked toward the gate.

"No, but he's weird. I think he has a thing about smells. When I was washing the bathroom the other day he kind of went nuts."

"What do you mean he went nuts?"

"He hissed and growled and then he sort did a flip."

Amanda laughed. Evelyn's heart thumped. She wasn't too far gone. She could still laugh. It was short lived, though. She straightened her face and said, "Let's go back. Your dad will be firing up the grill soon."

"No, wait. I want you to go to the rescue barn with me. Have you even seen Roan and Dapple?"

"Of course, I've seen them."

"Have you met them?"

Amanda looked at her daughter and smiled sadly. "Okay, let's go."

Jeff and Alice joined them a few minutes later. Evelyn had introduced Amanda to each of them and insisted that she stroke their soft muzzles.

"So, what do you think, Mom?" Alice asked. "Can Evelyn have them?"

"They'll just grow old and die. They all do." Her voice was almost a whisper. "But at least I won't have to watch it. I won't be here that long." She walked out of the barn. They watched her go. Her head was bowed. Her shoulders slumped.

"We've got a real problem," Evelyn said.

*

Evelyn breathed in the cool morning air on her way to work the next day. She shifted the large bag of drafting supplies to her other shoulder. It was heavier than she'd thought it was. These morning walks to work were so nice. The weather was cool these days.

Her spirits were a little dampened by her worry for her mother. They had sat around the pool and eaten dinner the night before. By the time she and Alice had left, Amanda's spirits had lifted a little bit.

Her dad had brought out the album of the twins as babies and they'd laughed over the chaos of raising two lively girls. Before the evening was over they had all taken a walk around the neighborhood. They'd avoided the stables this time but the two dogs had joined them.

When they left, Amanda had hugged both of her daughters and assured them that they didn't have to worry about her. Evelyn wanted to feel good about it, but she was a little bit afraid it was an act. Her mother didn't like to be the center of attention any more than she did.

She was surprised to see Jeff's car in the lot. He hadn't been coming in very much lately. She knew he was uncomfortable leaving Amanda.

"Hey, Dad." She dropped the bag in the chair in his office.

"Good morning, sweetie." He stood and walked around his desk to kiss her forehead.

"I'm surprised to see you. Is Mom okay at home alone?"

"Actually, I think your visit cheered her up some. She told me to stop hovering. Said I was getting on her nerves." He laughed. "When I left she was on her treadmill."

"That's a good sign. You said she'd stopped using her treadmill."

"Let's have a look at this office." He picked up the bag and went across the hall. "Do you want me to help you move anything around?"

"If you wouldn't mind. I'd like to have the drafting table over here in front of the window. But I'll help. I don't want you to mess up your knee."

"I don't really have to use my knee to move furniture but thanks for the concern." He laughed and went to the table. Evelyn moved to the other side of it and they positioned it in front of the window. The door to Darcy's office across the hall slammed and they exchanged a look.

"Did she just get here?" Evelyn asked. "I thought she came in at the crack of dawn."

"I did too." Jeff scowled. "I think I'm going to have a serious talk with her. This has gone far enough."

"Dad, don't. I'll handle it."

He looked back at her, but said nothing.

"I wanted to talk to you about something anyway. I'll get these things put away and come to your office in just a minute."

"Okay. I have some plans I can work on until you get there."

Evelyn set to work unpacking the supplies she'd brought. She'd bought her new desk the week before. It was supposed to be delivered today but in the meantime she could put her supplies on the shelf.

She stepped back to survey the room. It still looked very empty. She'd have to get some pictures for the wall or something. Her dad had framed some of his favorite plans and put them on the wall. He also had pictures of the finished product of some of his favorite jobs. Maybe someday she'd have the same thing. In the meantime she'd just have to get some pictures. She smiled to herself and turned to go.

"Oh!" She said, startled as she almost ran into Darcy. "I didn't hear you come in."

Darcy only looked at her for a minute then left the room. Evelyn sighed. Would things ever get better with the woman? She was really putting a damper on what should be a very exciting time in her life. She went on to her dad's office.

"I wanted to ask you about the corporate line of business?" She sat in the chair across from him. "Did that stop when Victoria left?"

"That was the last thing she did. She finished out all the contracts she had and didn't renew. I've never been interested in that end of the business. Decorating the inside of an office building just doesn't appeal to me."

"It appeals to me."

"I figured that was what you were getting at." He laughed. "It's yours if you want it, but I think that Vic said the competition was getting a little bit stiff. I don't know how easy it will be to break back into it."

"I'll have to look into that." She looked out the window of his office and saw a truck pull around back to the yard where they stacked the fertilizer and mulch. "That shipment of cow manure is in. I need to go."

"Honey, I've told you, you don't have to work on that sort of thing anymore."

"I want to, Dad. I've reorganized the yard. I need to make sure the guys keep to my plan until they're comfortable with the change."

Jeff leaned back in his chair and smiled. "Now you're talking like a pro."

*

"How was the pow wow with Daddy?"

Evelyn's shoulders tensed as she heard Darcy's voice behind her. She was reaching for a bag of manure but she stopped and turned around. "Your attitude is getting old, Darcy. If you want to talk to me, you'll have to change it. I'm not going to let you ruin any more of my days here. So why don't you just go bother someone else?" She turned back to reach for another bag.

"I guess you whined and wheedled until you talked him into giving you my storage room as your office."

Evelyn closed her eyes and counted to ten. She turned back around. "The office was his idea. But I think it's a good one. I didn't go to school for five years to be a stock boy."

Jason, one of the part time college students, tapped her on the shoulder as he climbed up onto the truck bed to pull the bags from the back. "What's wrong with being a stock boy?" He laughed.

"I'm a girl." She laughed back.

"Aren't you children cute," Darcy sneered. "Cute won't get you very far in this business. You won't succeed if you're not willing to get your hands dirty."

Evelyn held her gloved hands up in front of her. "They look pretty dirty to me." Darcy balled her fists, turned and stormed back to the building. Evelyn turned back to the truck to take the bag of manure that Jason was handing to her. The bag caught on a hook on the side of the truck, tore and sprayed cow poop all over her face. Luckily, she closed her eyes in time.

"I'm sorry, Ev." Jason jumped off the back of the truck and landed beside her.

She stood where she was for a minute then slowly wiped her lips with the back of her hand.

"Ev, are you alright?" A voice came from behind her and she cringed. It couldn't be. But it was. Jamie put his hands on her arms and turned her around.

"Why are you here at this particular moment?" She spit and looked around for a towel. Jason was hurrying toward her with one.

"Let me do that. My hands are clean." Jamie took the towel and wiped her mouth and then her eyes. She looked up at him. He was smiling. Actually, he was laughing. She stifled the urge to laugh back, afraid she would jolt him out of this candid moment.

"You're laughing at me," she said.

He stepped back and handed her the towel. "It was funny." The moment was gone.

She took the towel and headed to the greenhouse at the back of the yard. "There's a sink in here. I'll just clean up."

"I'll come with you." Jamie followed her.

"Why did you come here, Jamie?" She asked after she had washed her face. She avoided his eyes as she brushed at her shoulders and the front of her shirt.

"I came to see you. I wanted to apologize for being rude to you at Helen's party. I was out of line. I'm not a social butterfly you know." He laughed uncomfortably.

She looked at him then. He shuffled his feet and looked away.

"It's alright, Jamie," she said in what she hoped was a passive tone. "I think I've finally got the picture. You really don't want me anymore. You really don't love me. I'm a little thick but I've finally got it."

"Ev, it isn't like that, exactly."

"What is it like then, exactly?"

He shifted again, still avoiding her eyes. "It just isn't going to work. Our ages are too different. We come from different places in the world. It's just ..."

"... not going to work," she finished for him. "I think we've been over this. Like I said, Jamie, I've finally got it. Thanks for coming by. Apology accepted." She turned and busied herself with cleaning the manure out of the sink.

"Alright ... well ... I guess I'll see you then." She heard the door close behind him and waited a full minute before she let the tears go.

"I've got to go home and change my clothes. I had a little accident," she said from the door of Jeff's office.

"Pugh!" He waved a hand in front of his nose. "You sure did. Considering your track record, maybe you should bring a change of clothes with you every day." He laughed then stopped when he looked at her face. "What's wrong?"

"Nothing, Dad. Just let it go. I'll be back in a few minutes. Make that an hour. I want to shower and it's close enough to lunch time. I think I'll just spend it there with Sugar." Maybe Sugar would let her hold him and cry on his shoulder. She thought of the feisty kitten and smiled sadly. Or maybe not.

Chapter 5

Alice stood at the front door of the Parnell's three-bedroom brick ranch house. She remembered the place as always being a little crowded, but full of happy people. Jamie's dad was technician. She knew he worked on heating and air conditioning or something like that. His mom was a hairdresser.

Jamie had two sisters. The older one was a doctor; quite different than her parents. The younger one, Marisa, was planning to be a doctor. Jamie had struggled with some learning problems. She wasn't sure exactly what they were, but he could play tennis like a pro. In fact, she'd always wondered why he didn't go pro.

The door opened and she was looking at Jamie's mother. Meryl Parnell was a tall slender woman. Her hair was snowy white at this point and she wore it short. She stretched her arms out to Alice and pulled her into a warm embrace.

"Evelyn, I am so happy to see you. I was hoping you'd come to see me." She pulled her into the house and through the living room to the kitchen. "Sit down. I'm just brewing some tea. I'll get some cookies. We'll have a nice chat."

Alice sat down and caught her breath. She'd forgotten what a whirlwind of energy Jamie's mom was. She looked up when she realized that Meryl had stopped talking and was studying her closely.

"You look different." She shrugged and turned back to the counter to collect the teapot and cups. "I guess you've grown up since I saw you last."

"I've grown up some," Alice laughed. "But I think the reason I look different is probably because I'm Alice, not Evelyn."

Meryl whirled around. Alice jumped and laughed. The woman did everything fast. "You've cut your hair. I can't believe how much you and Evelyn look alike." She sat down across from her. "You know when you were growing up, your hair was always down to your waist. Evelyn's was always short. I knew you were twins, but I didn't realize how really identical you are. I'm sorry I mistook you."

"That's alright. It's not the first time that's happened. I hope you aren't too disappointed that I'm not Evelyn."

"No, of course not. I do wish she'd come to see me though. I don't feel comfortable calling her." She looked down as she poured the tea. "With things the way they are between her and Jamie."

"What's going on between her and Jamie?" Alice drizzled honey into her cup and stirred. "I guess you know that's why I'm here."

Meryl looked at Alice and smiled sadly. "I really can't talk to you about it. That would be a betrayal of Jamie's trust. As much as I love Evelyn, and you, Jamie is my son."

"I know. I didn't expect you to tell me anything about their relationship, but I was hoping you could tell me where he lives. I thought if I could talk to him in his own surroundings maybe I could get a little more understanding of the situation."

"I can't tell you that either. He's asked me not to tell anyone."

"Mrs. Parnel ..."

"Meryl."

"Meryl, Evelyn is miserable. She really loves him."

"I know. I'm sorry."

"Can you at least tell me if you think there is any hope for the relationship?"

"No."

"No. There's no hope for the relationship?"

"No. I can't tell you what I think about that."

Alice smiled inside and kept her features straight. She had unearthed a little bit of information. It seemed like Meryl still had some hope. "Evelyn says she's given up. She says she'll just have to adjust to life without him."

Meryl's face altered only slightly, but she was clearly saddened. "Alice," She looked up from her tea and into Alice's eyes. "I can't tell you much but I will say, Jamie isn't happy either. I do know and respect his motives. He does talk to me but ..." She smiled. "He doesn't listen to me."

Alice did smile that time. Meryl had just told her that he still loved Evelyn. Well, she'd just have to figure out a way to get them back together.

"If you can't tell me where he lives, can you give me his cell phone number?"

"No." Meryl leaned toward her. "But I can tell you that he's teaching at the country club this afternoon. He has four lessons, so he'll be there all afternoon." She leaned back. "I don't think that's too much information. Evelyn has already visited him there."

*

"Sir." Alice rounded her eyes at the guard in the gate house of the country club. "My father will kill me if I'm late to this luncheon. He'll be so mad that I still haven't put the pass sticker on my car. I just keep forgetting. Please, Please, Please, give me a temporary pass." She hoped he didn't remember Evelyn pulling the same thing a few weeks ago.

"Well, alright." She noticed him eyeing the Porsche convertible enviously. "But you be sure to put that sticker on as soon as you get home. Not all the guards are as nice as I am." He handed her the pass and she pulled away. She followed the signs to the tennis courts and pulled into a parking space.

As she got out of her car she turned at the sound of a car door closing. Across the parking lot, almost hidden by the dumpster, Jamie was walking away from the most decrepit looking jalopy she had ever seen. She looked around the parking lot. There were a couple of other Porsches there. Hopefully he wouldn't recognize hers. She didn't think she wanted him to know she was here just yet.

He disappeared around the side of the tennis shop. Alice waited a few seconds then went across the parking lot to get a good look at the car. It was an old hatch back of some kind. There were no identifying emblems of any kind on it, just holes where they used to be. There was no rear window. A piece of clear but cloudy plastic was stretched across it and secured with blue tape.

She glanced around to make sure that no one was near then looked in the window. The only seat in the car was the driver's seat. On the passenger side was a tool box, the kind that doubles as a stool. In place of the back seat was a large trunk. She tried the passenger side door, but it was locked.

"Oh, come on, Jamie," she said to herself. "Who's going to steal this car?"

She tried to slide her hand through the plastic on the hatch, but the tape was surprisingly strong. She went around to the driver's side door. It was locked too. The window was slightly open at the top, but she was sure she couldn't get anything but her fingers through it. She pushed them through anyway and felt the window slide slightly further down. She pushed gently until it was completely open.

"Woah, Jamie," she murmured. "You're really poor." Surely they paid him enough at the university to drive a better car than this.

She unlocked the door and looked for a lever to open the hatch. There wasn't one. Maybe cars that old didn't have levers. She walked around to the back and found a button to push that released the hatch. Carefully she raised it and looked inside. She lifted the lid on the trunk. It was very dark in the shade of the trees and the dumpster. You couldn't see the bottom of the trunk. She put her hand inside carefully hoping there wasn't some kind of creature in there. It was empty. Hmmmm. He must keep his tennis equipment in it.

She closed the hatch and returned to the driver's seat door. Leaving the door unlocked, she grasped the window with both hands and gently pulled it back up. She had an idea, but she couldn't leave and come back in four hours. Besides, she needed to think it through. There was tennis and golf, yuck. The pool was closed for winter. She looked around for signs. Indoor racquetball courts, no. Spa! That's it. She'd spend the afternoon in the spa. She hurried back to her car to get her pass.

*

Jamie pulled down the long gravel driveway of his property. He stopped under the makeshift carport he had built and got out of the car. It had been a long day. He'd been up at the crack of dawn to go to his job at the university. He'd had more classes than usual because he was filling in for Don. They'd taken a long weekend to visit Helen's parents.

Then he'd gone directly to the country club and taught four lessons in a row. One of the students had a crush on him. He wasn't being conceited. In fact, he hated it. The girl was doing everything she could to get his attention including flashing cleavage, up high and down low. He shivered.

The young boy he'd just started teaching was a typical spoiled rich kid. He wouldn't listen to anything Jamie told him and took great pleasure in hitting the balls over the fence so that Jamie had to retrieve them. He'd tried making the kid do it but the brat refused so that by the end of the hour all fifty of Jamie's tennis balls were in the field. It took him another half hour to collect them before he could go home. In the end he'd come up five short, like he could really afford to buy new tennis balls.

He popped the hatch on the car and opened the trunk to retrieve his racket.

"What took you so long?" Alice sat up and handed him his racket.

Jamie jumped back in surprise.

"You know you should be more careful with your racket. The way you tossed it into the trunk you could have broken it, not to mention the bruise you put on me." She rubbed her shoulder as she climbed out of the car.

"Alice, what were you doing in there?"

"Suffocating. I'm glad I took the latch off. I think I'd have smothered in there if I hadn't." She straightened her pants and shirt and looked up at him. "Hey, how did you know I wasn't Evelyn? I cut my hair. We're identical."

"Not quite," he said and leaned into the car to gather his tennis balls and duffel bag. "Now will you please tell me why you were hiding in the trunk of my car?"

"The trunk of your car, that's funny. I think it's more like the trunk in your car." She laughed then sobered. "Jamie, why are you driving this heap? Surely the school pays you more than that." She looked around and sobered even more. She'd known the driveway was gravel by the roughness of the trip down it. But the property was pure jungle. They were in a clearing about the size of a couple of tennis courts. It was fenced all the way around. There were two large metal structures at one end of it. She and Jamie were standing under a car port just big enough for one small car. Next to that was a small wooden hut. It was probably about ten feet by ten feet and not nearly as high. Beyond the clearing the forest was so thick she couldn't see through it.

"Where are we, Jamie?"

"We're at my palace. Can't you tell?" He started toward the hut. He stopped and turned with his hand on the door knob. "Wait here for just a minute. I'll take you home after I do a couple of things. You know, I really didn't want to drive back into town tonight. I've had a long day." He ducked and went through the door.

Alice looked around again. She was about to get up the nerve to go down to the other buildings when Jamie came back out the door. He'd changed out of his tennis shorts. He wore jeans and a t-shirt and was holding a pair of work boots in his hand. He sat down on a tree stump to put them on.

"Jamie," Alice asked. "How tall are you?"

"Six two. Why?"

"How high is the ceiling on that building?"

He rolled his eyes. "It's probably about six feet, maybe less."

"Definitely less. Why don't you live in one of those buildings? They look like mobile homes."

"They are mobile homes." He stood and started toward the buildings.

"Why do you live in a hut that's too short for you when you could live in a mobile home?" She hurried behind him, jogging to keep up with his long strides.

Just as they reached the first building a siren sounded in the distance and the entire building erupted in a chorus of howls.

Alice stopped in her tracks. "There are dogs in there."

"That's right, and I have to feed them and turn them out before we can go."

*

"You'll have to drive, Alice."

"Why?" They were about to head back to town. Alice had followed Jamie silently through his obviously well-established routine of feeding a mobile home full of dogs and then one full of cats. He'd had to let the dogs out in the run then put them all away again. She hadn't said a word. She was speechless.

"You have to drive because there's only one seat belt."

She looked into the driver's side window. "There's only one seat. I can fit into the trunk better than you."

"I'll sit on the tool box."

"You trust me to drive your car?"

"I don't care about the car. I want you to have the seat belt. All I need is for you to get hurt in my car."

"You're not worried about me." She laughed as she got into the driver's seat and buckled up. "You're worried about what Ev would think of you if I got hurt."

"Not so much Ev, your father. He has to work at not killing me as it is."

She looked at him surprised and turned the key. "Dad likes you. All fathers are a little bit jealous of their daughter's boyfriends, but he always liked you."

"Maybe." He arranged himself on the tool box. His knees were under his chin.

"So where are we, Jamie. Which way do I go?" She looked both ways on the highway that the driveway ran off.

"That's right." He laughed for the first time all day. "You came in a trunk. I don't know why I didn't see you when I put my racquet in. Turn left."

"I hid under a dark towel. Answer my question; where are we?"

"We're just a little south of Atlanta. I got a good deal on some land down here. Things sell for less in this area than in North Atlanta. It's a shame really, because the countryside is beautiful."

"All I saw was jungle." She saw the sign for the interstate and pulled onto the northbound ramp.

"Jungle's beautiful."

"I guess so." They sat in uncomfortable silence for a moment. "Tell me the story, Jamie, the whole story, the truth and nothing but the truth."

"I don't lie, Alice." He looked out the window. The sun had gone down. There was nothing to see but the highway lights.

"No, but sometimes you withhold information."

"I guess there isn't any point in withholding it now." He laughed, but it wasn't a happy laugh. "You've found me out."

"Yeah, so start talking."

"I just made a big mistake and now I'm stuck with it."

"What mistake? Come on, I'm not going to let up until I understand what's going on."

"It isn't the reason I cooled things off with Evelyn. I mean in a way it is but not really. I thought that after she went away to school she needed some space. She needed to know what her options were. She's got a lot going for her. She doesn't need to saddle herself with a tennis coach."

"I don't think she'd have a problem with a tennis coach at all, but it isn't a small thing to be on the faculty of a major university, even if it is on the tennis team."

"Yeah, well, that's not going to happen."

"Stop talking in riddles, Jamie. Tell me why you're living in a hut that's smaller than you when you have dogs and cats in real houses."

"Mobile homes."

"Mobile homes are real houses."

"Okay, okay. For the first couple of years after Ev went away, I was working on getting my bachelor's degree in Physical Education. I was working at the school teaching tennis. I was doing pretty well. I had the hope scholarship and with the help of good friends and tutors, I was able to hold on to it. You know I have some learning issues."

"I know. You're ADD."

"Yeah that's right, and I have some mild dyslexia. I hate it."

"They called me ADD in school. It's no big deal."

"It didn't slow you down though."

"Nothing slows me down." She laughed.

"No, but slow the car down." He laughed too. This time it sounded better. "Don't forget I'm sitting on a tool box."

"Don't try to change the subject."

"I actually saved some money. I was living at home with Mom and Dad. Then I made a friend at school and moved out to share an apartment with him. After a while I could even afford to have my own place."

"With an apartment and all the expenses you were still saving money? You manage money better than I do."

"I actually surprised myself. I did a lot of teaching tennis on the side. Those rich folks at the country club pay well. So ... I guess I got a little bit of a swollen head. You know I've done volunteer work at the animal shelter. I've always admired the rescue work that your mom and dad do. I had this dream of having my own rescue facility."

"Looks like to me you're making that dream come true."

"It seemed that way at first. Like I said, I got this great deal on this property. It was a foreclosure. I never could have bought it otherwise. I had enough to put a down payment on it but there's a hefty mortgage. It didn't seem that hefty at first, but it did after I'd bought the units for the animals. And of course, the units have to be air conditioned. The guys can't live inside in the heat. The cold isn't as bad but they can't survive in those buildings in the heat. Then there's the food. I've managed to get a couple of vets to give me discounts. I have some vet techs that volunteer time, but with everything else I do ... Well ... I'm in over my head, Alice. I can't keep up with it all."

He sounded defeated. Alice couldn't say anything for a minute. There had to be a way for him to make this dream a reality. "Couldn't you get a small business loan? You could use the money to build kennels. Then you could make enough money keeping people's pets to support the rescue." She was thrilled with her idea. Why hadn't he thought of it himself?

"I thought of that. They wanted a prospectus. That's a paper you write up to tell them how you're going to make enough money to pay them back. I'm no good at that kind of thing, writing I mean. I didn't make the cut."

"Did you get someone to help you write it? You didn't mind getting help in school."

"I don't want anyone to know about this mess. Mom's the only one that knows any of this."

"I know. I talked to her today." She felt Jamie tense next to her. "She didn't tell me anything," she said quickly. "She just said that you talk to her and she couldn't betray your trust by telling me anything."

"That's good. I'd hate to have to be mad at her. She's pretty much all I've got at this point."

Evelyn pulled the car off the highway and headed toward the country club.

"Why are we going this way?" Jamie asked.

"My car is parked at the shopping center across from the country club."

"I guess some planning went into the little stunt you pulled today."

"I'll tell you about it some time." She laughed. "Jamie, why don't you use your income for collateral for a loan? Surely, you make enough at the university to qualify for a loan."

"I'm just an assistant coach. I don't make enough."

"I thought you were going to be faculty after you finished graduate school. When will that happen?"

"It won't. I didn't qualify for graduate school."

"I thought you said your grades were good. You have to maintain a B average to get the hope scholarship."

"I had an A average, 3.6 to be exact. I bombed the boards."

"Oh, man!" She pulled into the parking spot next to her car and got out. Jamie came around the car and stood next to her.

"I suppose you'll have to tell Evelyn all of this."

She looked up at him. His face was in shadow. She couldn't see his expression. "I don't have to. I won't."

"Yes, you will. I know the way the two of you are. She'll know there's something going on and you'll end up telling her. I guess it was stupid of me to try to keep it quiet. It's just embarrassing, that's all."

"Don't be embarrassed, and don't do anything drastic until I have time to think about this for a while. There has to be a way."

"I'm not going in on one of your harebrained schemes."

"My schemes aren't harebrained." She stood on her toes and kissed his cheek. "Be careful going home. And don't bump your head on the ceiling when you get up in the morning."

Jamie laughed as he slid behind the wheel. He backed out of the parking space. The car backfired as he pulled away.

*

"You're here early." David turned from his desk in the office they shared in the café above the nursery.

Alice set her bag on her desk and sat down. She cleared a space on the surface and rummaged through the drawer looking for a pen and note pad.

"You know you really should try to organize that desk. I don't know how you work over there."

"It may look disorganized but I know where everything is. Can I borrow a pen?" She held out her hand.

"You know where everything is except your pen."

"Actually, I know where my pen is too. It's at home."

David laughed and pulled a pen from the holder on his neat desk. "So why are you here so early?" He looked at his clock. "It's only 10:30. That's got to be a record. Even with the new lunch hours, you usually don't get here until after we start serving."

"I wanted to get a start on a few new specials I plan for the week day dinner menu." She wrote something down on her pad.

David turned back to his desk. "I'm working on the books. We're doing great. I'm excited. I'm glad you brought me in on this little venture."

Alice tapped her pen on the desk in front of her and looked at the back of her cousin's head. She'd known David all her life. He'd been in his mid-twenties when she and Evelyn were born. His dad had been an absentee father until David was grown. Then he'd come back into his life. They seemed to have mended any fences they'd broken, but her own father had raised him really, he and David's mom. She had died the previous summer.

"How's your dad, David. I know he took your mom's death pretty hard."

"He's a mess." He turned back around. His expression had changed from cheerful to concern. "You know they had resumed their relationship after his divorce. I think he had a long happy retirement planned with her. The cancer came so suddenly and took her so fast, he didn't have a chance to adjust at all. Not that you can adjust to that kind of thing. He just seems to walk around in a daze all the time. He's letting his health go. I've tried but I can't seem to get through to him. I just don't know what's going to happen."

He turned back to his work and Alice studied the back of his head. She tapped her pen on the desk to the rhythm of Auld Lang Syne and thought about her own mother, how sad she was. What would it be like to lose her? How would her dad make it without her? What a terrible thought. Her thoughts turned to Evelyn and Jamie. They were so in love with each other. Would they ever work it out? Neither one of them was going to die anytime soon, but still what a waste of precious time.

"Alice," David said without turning around. "You're distracting me with that tapping. It isn't new years you know. And please stop staring a hole in the back of my head."

"I'm sorry." She looked down at her paper. She'd written rescue on her paper. What did that have to do with dinner specials? "David, your best friend is James Parnell, right?"

"You know he is." He turned around. "We've been best friends since grade school. Why?"

"You tutored his son Jamie in school, didn't you?"

"Yes, but if you're digging for info on Jamie, you're in the wrong place. I would never betray my best friend's trust by revealing confidences between us. But even if I would, I can't. I don't know anything. Jimmy doesn't know anything. He's worried sick about the kid. Meryl won't tell him anything except that Jamie is safe. She says she can't betray young James's trust. It's really complicated."

"I think it's about to come out in the open. All the secrecy, I mean. I kind of busted him last night."

"What do you mean? You're not going to tell me you can't betray his trust, are you?"

"Why is it alright for you to say it to me and not the other way around?"

"It isn't but tell me anyway."

Alice laughed. "I love you, David."

"I love you too." He leaned forward. "So, what did you do, and what did you find out?"

"Okay, I'll tell you but you can't betray my trust."

They laughed.

"Really, David, I'm pretty sure Jamie is going to come clean to his family now. He expects me to tell Ev, but I told him I wouldn't. Of course, the only way to do that is to not see her until it's all out. She can always tell when I'm keeping something from her."

"Well, I can keep it from her. Tell me."

She told him the story from beginning to end. He laughed through most of it. But he sobered at the end.

"I shouldn't have laughed about his hut. It's really kind of sad, but you have to admit his ceiling being shorter than him has some humor to it."

"He even laughed about it. The car is funny too. But the fact that he's that poor isn't. David, those dogs live in nice accommodations. They even have indoor plumbing. He has to go to the kennels to use the bathroom."

"What does he plan to do?"

"He doesn't know what to do. He had big plans, you know, to build kennels with runs. I think he said he has twenty acres. He was even going to do some horse rescue. But he's out of money."

"Couldn't he get a small business loan?"

"No. He doesn't qualify."

David leaned back and studied Alice. She squirmed a little and looked down to doodle on her pad.

"There's more to this story, isn't there."

"That's pretty much all I can tell you. Really, please don't talk to anyone about this until Jamie's had time to talk to his family. It really needs to come from him."

"I can see what you mean. I'm not going to ask why the secrecy. Young James has always been proud, maybe a little too proud. I just wonder if there's any way I can help him. His heart is in the right place."

"Yeah, but right now we just have to sit tight."

*

Alice scanned the nursery as she came down the stairs a few days later. She had managed to avoid Evelyn since her visit with Jamie. She knew she could try not to tell her what she'd found out, but Evelyn would know something was going on. She just felt she needed to give Jamie some more time. She hadn't heard anything from him and she really didn't expect to. There had to be another way to find out if he'd told his family. Maybe she could have lunch with Marisa. Evelyn and she were becoming friends. Why couldn't they be a threesome? She'd never really liked Marisa that much, of course. Her family had spoiled her. She was considerably younger than her brother and sister, and she was kind of a goody goody. She'd have to think of something else.

"Evelyn, wait." Alice heard someone call. She turned around thinking that her sister must be somewhere close by if someone was calling to her. She scanned the room but saw no sign of Evelyn. Then she noticed a pretty redhead with a loaded cart. She was waving to her from behind a display. It was a case of mistaken identity. Alice looked around again. Evelyn could come in any minute, but she couldn't just ignore the woman. Resigned, she went to greet her.

"Evelyn," the woman said. "I'm glad I caught you. Lindsey said you were gone for the day."

"Lindsey?" Alice asked.

"You know, the cashier." She laughed. "I'm in here so often we've become friends. Anyway, I wanted to talk to you about Jamie. I wondered if he'd talked to you lately. He said he was going to apologize for being rude to you at the party. And ... well ... he has some news."

For just a second Alice considered not revealing who she was. Maybe she could find out if Jamie had come clean this way. Of course, that would be wrong. No. She couldn't do that.

"I'm sorry," she said. "You've mistaken me for my sister. I'm Evelyn's twin. I'm Alice."

"Wow, you two really are identical twins." She held out her hand. "I'm Helen Morris. I work with Jamie at the university. Evelyn and I have become friends. She's confided in me a little bit about her relationship with Jamie."

Alice was relieved to know that Evelyn had gone home. She looked down at the full cart. "You love your garden, I see."

"Yes, I do. But I must admit that I came here today to talk to Evelyn. I wondered if she was getting anywhere with Jamie." She looked sad for a minute. "My husband and I have always been close to him. But lately he's so distant. I don't think he's very happy. I was hoping Evelyn could help with that."

She didn't know what Jamie's news had been, but he obviously hadn't told Helen about Alice's little visit.

"We were all hoping, but the last time I talked to her she said she was going to give up on him. If he was working so hard at pushing her away he must really not want her."

Helen looked seriously at Alice. "Do you believe that?"

"No."

"What are we going to do about it?" Helen pulled her cart toward the cashier. Alice walked along beside her.

"I haven't figured that out yet. But I'll come up with something."

*

Alice put her keys on the cluttered table beside her front door and tossed her purse on the couch. She looked around the room. The place really needed to be cleaned but she'd taken the night off to relax and watch a movie. Cleaning would have to wait.

The new assistant manager she'd hired was working out well. The woman was probably about ten years older than Alice. At first, managing someone older than her was a little bit intimidating but Alice never stayed intimidated for long. She was only twenty-three. She'd finished culinary school at twenty and had been working the night shift at the café ever since. It was her place, well, hers and David's. She'd done the nightshift all by herself until now. She was ready to have more than one day off a week. David had had an assistant manager from the start, but then it wasn't his first career.

She went to the kitchen to pour herself a glass of lemonade. It was a taste she had inherited from her dad. She smiled when she thought of him. He was such an old sweetheart.

She cleared a spot on the couch, stretched out and picked up the remote. Before she had a chance to hit the button her cell phone rang. Oh no, she thought. She'd forgotten to take it to work with her. Where could it be in all this mess? She followed the sound until she found it under a pile of clean laundry.

"Hello?"

"Alice." Her father's voice was strained. "Your mother's been in an accident. I'm at St. Joseph's hospital. I need you here."

Her whole body hummed as she grabbed her keys and ran out the door.

Chapter 6

Jeff sat beside Amanda's hospital bed. He'd been holding her hand for what seemed like hours. Her face was so pale. One of her arms was in a cast. She'd broken it above and below the elbow. They'd had her in surgery for an hour. She'd ruptured her spleen. and they'd removed it. She had never cried. Her eyes had expressed her pain. They'd given her something for it. She was sleeping now.

"Dad." Evelyn whispered as she peered into the darkened room.

Jeff released Amanda's hand and hurried toward his daughter. He wrapped his arms around her and lowered his cheek to the top of her head.

She wrapped her arms around her father's waist and buried her face in his chest. She felt more than heard his sobs. Her dad was a passionate man. She'd seen him cry many times over the deaths of their animals, over the loss of his friends. But these tears were different. She could feel the fear, the desperation.

They both moved slightly as they felt Alice join them from the doorway. The three of them stood like that, wrapped in each other's arms for a few minutes. Then Jeff stepped back, not releasing them but loosening his hold.

"How is she?"

"What happened?"

They all three moved to the bed and looked down at Amanda.

"She was just going to the grocery store. I thought it was good because she wouldn't let me come with her. She said I was hovering. She said she was about to get fed up. She was acting like her old self again. I shouldn't have let her go alone."

"It's not your fault, Dad." Evelyn put her hand on his arm.

"I was in the barn with Doris. I've been a little worried about the old girl. My cell phone rang. It's a miracle I had it with me, I rarely remember it. It was the hospital. All they would tell me was that she'd been in an accident and I needed to come here."

"They didn't even tell you if she was okay?"

"They said she was serious but stable."

"Did someone hit her?" Evelyn asked. "Mom is such a careful driver. I can't believe it could have been her fault."

"It was a one car accident. The policeman said she'd driven off the road on Old Evan's Mill. You know where the creek is dammed to make that small lake. She almost went into it. Thank God she didn't."

They stood in silence, all thinking the same thing. Evelyn put her hand on her mother's shoulder. A tear rolled down her cheek and splashed onto the sheet. "Dad," she whispered. "You don't think she …"

"No!" Amanda's eyes opened and she looked from one of them to the other. "I didn't do it on purpose!"

*

"When am I going to learn to keep my mouth shut?" Evelyn sat in the waiting area of the hospital.

"We were all thinking it, Ev." Alice put her arm across her sister's shoulders.

"Yes, but who said it, and right in front of her. I'm stupid. I'm just plain stupid."

"We thought she was asleep."

"I still shouldn't have said it. Like I said, I'm stupid."

"You're the smart sister, Ev, remember? Magna Cum Laude." Alice laughed and looked in the direction of Amanda's room. After Evelyn had apologized for thinking such a thing, and for almost saying such a thing, Jeff had ushered them out of the room for a minute alone with Amanda. She was agitated. If anyone could calm her down he could.

He appeared in the doorway and motioned them to come back. They hurried toward the room.

"Mom." Evelyn ran to the bed and took her mother's hand. Amanda turned her head to look the other way. "Mom, please forgive me. It's just that I love you so much. We've been so worried about you." The tears ran down her face and she hiccoughed.

Amanda turned back to her and smiled weakly. "I guess I'm just embarrassed."

"Don't be embarrassed, Mom." Alice stepped to the other side of the bed and smoothed her mother's hair. "Remember when Evelyn drove her car through the fence and into the barn."

"I didn't drive it there." Evelyn was getting agitated now. Why was she always the butt of all the jokes? Why did they always call her clumsy? Why didn't they call Alice clumsy? Because Alice wasn't clumsy. She took a deep breath. Now was not the time to be thinking about herself.

"And remember the time when you were teaching her to drive." Alice continued, "You told her to turn left but she turned right instead. Unfortunately, there wasn't a road there. She hit a fire hydrant."

Jeff and Alice laughed. Evelyn smiled self-consciously. Amanda laughed then sucked in her breath. She pulled her hand away from Evelyn's and clutched her side.

"So, what's the damage, Jeff?" She did sound more like her old self again. Evelyn smiled and Alice smoothed her mother's hair back again.

"They had to remove your spleen," he said, taking her hand again. "The doctor says you'll do fine without it. You have a compound fracture of your left arm. It's a good thing you're right handed. He says it should heal okay."

"When can I go home?"

"In a day or two. They don't keep people in the hospital for long these days. It costs too much."

"I want to go home now."

"You had some head trauma, Manda. They want to keep an eye on you for at least another day. But I'll stay with you. I couldn't sleep at home without you anyway."

"Who will take care of the horses?" Amanda's voice wavered. "What about the dogs and the chickens?"

"I'll stay out there," Evelyn said.

"You can't leave Sugar." Amanda's eyes were swimming with tears.

"I'll stay out there," Alice said. "I don't have any ties at home. I haven't stayed at the house for a while. It'll be fun."

Amanda put her hand on Alice's. "Thank you, honey. I really do want Dad to stay with me. I hate hospitals. I hate being away from home."

Alice smiled and leaned down to kiss her mother's cheek.

Evelyn wasn't sure what she felt but it wasn't comfortable. Was she such a selfish person that she couldn't put her mother's feelings before her own? She didn't know. Something was churning inside her head. She had a feeling she was going to embarrass herself.

*

Evelyn sat at the kitchen table in her family home. She braced herself for the confrontation she expected with her sister. Alice's car had just pulled into the four car garage. The door had slammed. She was on her way to the kitchen.

"What are you doing here?" Alice demanded when she came through with her overnight case. "It was decided that I would stay here and take care of the animals."

"It was decided by you and Mom. I guess she doesn't think I'm capable."

"What's your problem, Ev? She didn't question your capability. You know how she is with the animals. She was worried about your cat."

"Like he can't stay alone overnight. Like I won't remember to feed him when I go to work tomorrow."

Suddenly there was a hissing sound from the doorway. A white blur launched itself at Alice's leg and latched on.

"Ahhh …" She screamed and tried to shake Sugar off. "I thought you said you could leave him overnight."

Evelyn pried Sugar off Alice's leg and kissed him. She put him on the floor. He hissed and batted at Alice's foot.

"Why does he hate me?"

"He doesn't. He's protecting me. You were acting aggressive toward me when you came in the door."

"I didn't mean to attack you." Alice stepped back to put some distance between herself and the angry cat. "You know, Ev, I think that cat's dangerous."

"Are you bleeding? Do you feel any pain?"

Alice looked down at her leg and her foot. "No, now that you mention it. His paws were soft and he didn't bite."

"He's a good boy." Evelyn rubbed her hand along the cat's back and he arched. "And since he seems to be the only person that has any faith in me, I wanted to bring him along."

"I don't know what you're talking about."

"Do you have any idea what it's like to be your little sister?"

"You're talking crazy, Ev. We're only twelve minutes apart. We're the same age."

"You didn't think it was insignificant growing up. In fact, you reminded me of it all the time. You were always in front. You were always a little taller than me. You always weighed a little more."

"Okay now you're getting nasty."

"I mean at the yearly checkups. You were more athletic. I was always too clumsy. Nobody wanted to play with me. You even blew out all the candles on our birthday cake. I never got to blow out a single one."

Alice stood with her mouth open for just a second. "You always wanted me to blow out those candles. You said you didn't like being the center of attention."

"Maybe that's because I knew I couldn't compete with you. I just decided not to try."

"Ev." Alice put her hand on Evelyn's shoulder. "I didn't know you felt that way. Why haven't you said anything before now?"

"Because I don't feel that way. I did want you to blow out all the candles. You're right I'm talking crazy. I must be going crazy."

"Well, there has to be some truth to what you just said. Otherwise it wouldn't have come tumbling out like it did."

"I rehearsed it in my head."

They laughed. Evelyn reached down and picked up the confused kitten. He purred and rubbed his face on her chin.

"So why are you feeling so low? Is it Jamie? Is Darcy getting to you? The other day when I talked to Dad he said he was really proud of your work. He thinks you're doing great."

"I'm adjusting to being without Jamie. You know, I really thought that when I came home I could bring him around. I guess he really doesn't love me. That hurts but I'm adjusting.

Alice didn't say anything.

"I don't know what I'm going to do about Darcy. She's just not coming around. I thought she would but she seems determined to hate me. I really have to make an effort to not let her get in my way."

"I think Dad should fire her."

"That isn't the answer. Dad doesn't want to do all the management stuff. I don't either."

"Hire someone else to do it."

"I suppose we could, but Darcy has done a good job for so many years. I didn't think that when I got out of school and started at the nursery I would disrupt things so much. I didn't want to. I thought I'd just slide right in. It's what I've always wanted. It's what I've planned for all my life. I guess I'm just spoiled. Everything can't be that easy."

"You're no more spoiled than I am." They looked at each other and dissolved into laughter.

"Okay." Alice rubbed her eyes. "We're both a little bit spoiled. Maybe things have been easy for us. Mom and Dad always made sure we had just what we wanted. But that doesn't mean we give up when things get a little bit hard."

"You don't. That's what's bothering me right now. Look at you. You were born with a heart problem. You had surgery on your first day. It didn't slow you down. You were always the most dynamic of us. Captain of the cheerleading team. First place in the gymnastics meets. I roll sideways when I try to do a summersault. See, nothing was handed to you. You went out and got it. I just followed Dad around playing in the dirt."

"Let me just remind you that you were the captain of the debate team. You were valedictorian of our high school graduating class. You graduated from college Magna Cum laude."

"I was a nerd."

"And I was Miss Popularity. Those were the parts we played and we played them well."

"I didn't realize we were playing parts. I don't think I know my lines anymore."

"You're really feeling low. I'm sorry."

"I'm probably just feeling sorry for myself." She stood and went to the refrigerator. "There isn't any food in here. Speaking of feeling low, Mom is scaring me. I don't ever remember coming home to an empty fridge."

Alice looked into the refrigerator over her shoulder. "We'll go to the store after we feed the horses tomorrow morning. Right now, let's order a pizza."

*

Evelyn woke up in the bed she'd slept in as a child. It was a pleasant familiar feeling to look out the window onto the gracefully landscaped yard. She'd always loved that. Her dad changed the landscaping all the time but there was a certain sameness to it. It had his signature on it. She'd slept with her window open. It was early October. The evenings were cool. The mornings were cooler. But with a warm comforter and a flannel sheet it was nice to wake to the cool country air.

She pushed back the covers and shivered as she went to the window to close it. From her upstairs window she could see the front of the property. She could only see the very top of the barn but the pasture that Doris and Elmo shared was visible beyond the barn. She laughed. Elmo was nuzzling Doris as she lay on the ground. Poor old horse, Evelyn thought. I guess she sleeps in these days.

Then her heart started to pound. Doris was lying just a little bit too still. Elmo pushed her leg with his nose. It didn't move.

"Alice," Evelyn called as she pulled on her jeans. "Oh my god, Alice." She ran out of the room almost bouncing off her sister in the hall.

"What is it? What's wrong?"

"Doris is down, Alice. I've got a bad feeling."

The two of them ran down the stairs and out the door. Evelyn didn't realize she was barefoot until she hit the driveway. She didn't care. Alice opened the gate and they bolted through. Evelyn skidded to a stop on her knees at the horse's head. Alice stood behind her with her hand to her mouth.

The body was cold. "She was fine when I fed her last night. I mean she was hobbling around when I let her out. I just thought it was because she was old. Maybe I should have put her in her stall. It was a cool night."

"She could have gone to her stall, Ev. It's not your fault. She was an old horse."

"I hope she didn't suffer."

"She isn't suffering anymore if she did." Alice sank to her knees and put her hand on the horse's side. "She's cold but she isn't stiff. I don't know what that means."

"Me neither." Evelyn's voice hitched as the lump in her throat gave way to the tears in her eyes. She sniffled and wiped the back of her hand across her cheek.

"She's been here all our lives." Alice leaned forward and put her face in her hands as she started to cry. Evelyn put her hand on Alice's shoulder. They moved into each other's arms and cried together until Elmo nudged Evelyn on the shoulder.

"Oh, Elmo." They both got to their feet and put their arms around the mule's neck. "What will you do now?" Alice said.

"She didn't die alone." Evelyn sniffed. "At least she didn't die alone. Elmo was with her."

They stood looking down at the still form of the horse they'd known all their lives. They'd learned to ride on her, Doris and Sarge. Their parents had both had a horse when they were growing up. Sarge had been a gentle giant. Doris had been a little more lively but never mean. She'd loved the kids and they'd loved her.

"What now?" Evelyn sniffled.

"I don't know. I guess we'd better call Dad. I don't think they'll discharge Mom today, but if they do, he needs to tell her before they get home."

"Yeah, does he have his cell with him?"

"I think so. He said that was how they reached him about the accident. I think I'll put Elmo in his stall."

They both looked back at the mule. He stood over the body of his friend.

"Leave him. It looks like he's guarding her. I think he needs a little more time."

"You're probably right." They linked arms and walked slowly back to the house.

*

The two of them took the next day off. Jeff had been heart broken when they told him about Doris. But he was able to tell them what to do. They were to call the rescue service that he worked with. They provided a cremation service and they would pick up the body.

It was lucky that they could arrange it for the next day. Amanda would come home from the hospital that afternoon and they wanted the body gone when she did.

"Dad says she didn't even shed a tear." Alice hung up the phone. "He said before he told her about Doris she seemed to be coming around. After he told her she just crawled back inside herself. She hasn't said much since. Evelyn what are we going to do?"

"I don't know. She'll never accept treatment and she's only getting worse."

"They'll be here any minute. Put the flowers on the table and smile."

They both stood when they heard the garage door go up. "Welcome home," they said together as Jeff helped Amanda through the door.

"We cooked dinner," Evelyn said. "I hope you're hungry."

"I couldn't eat anything," Amanda said as she headed for the back staircase. "I think I'll just lie down."

"Manda, don't go up the stairs. Why don't you lie down in the living room?"

"Yeah, Mom," Evelyn said. "I'll bring you a tray. We fixed your favorite, lamb chops."

Her mother looked back at her with sad eyes. "At least Doris didn't die so I could eat her."

"We're sorry, Mom." Alice stepped forward and gently put her arm around her mother. "We didn't think about that."

"It's not your fault, honey. I just need to go to bed for a while."

"You've been in bed for two days, Manda." Jeff put the flowers that he had brought from the hospital on the table with the others. "Look what the girls have done for you. Please stay and eat something."

She looked at the flowers and then at the girls. "Thank you, babies, but I need to lie down. Maybe later." She turned again toward the steps.

"Manda, you shouldn't be climbing steps."

"Jeff, there is nothing wrong with my legs. I broke my arm, remember?" She turned and climbed the stairs.

"She snapped at me. Maybe that's a good thing."

"Well, I hope you'll eat something, Dad. We made a feast."

"You bet I will. Hospital food is awful. We had no food here before the accident. That's why she was going to the grocery store." He opened the refrigerator and gasped. "You stocked up. Thanks, girls. I should give you some money."

"It's okay. We used the credit card in the top left-hand drawer of your dresser."

"You knew about that card?"

"We've always known about that card."

*

When Evelyn got to work the next morning Jeff's truck was in the parking lot. She went directly to her office to put away her things. Then she tiptoed past Darcy's office and knocked on Jeff's door.

"Are you sure you should have left Mom?" She asked as she sat down in the chair across from him.

"I was getting on her nerves. Besides, I think it's important to let her know that I trust her."

"Especially after I opened my big mouth."

"Don't worry about that, sweetie. Now listen. I want to show you something in the back greenhouse. I've tried to create a hybrid of some tulips. I'm not having any luck. Maybe since you're right out of school you can tell me what I'm doing wrong."

"It's probably because tulips aren't native. They need a cooler climate."

"I refuse to accept that."

Evelyn laughed as she followed him out the door. "You've always had a hard time accepting limitation."

He put his arm across her shoulders. They went through the shop toward the back yard. Darcy was on the loading dock checking off a shipment. She looked in their direction, scowled, and looked back down at her clipboard.

"Good morning, Darcy," Jeff called cheerfully. "Is that the shipment of mulch?"

"Yes, it is." She answered sourly.

"How's that new vender working out?"

"Fine." She didn't look up from her clipboard.

Jeff guided Evelyn around the dock and onto the path that went past the greenhouses. "I think she forgets who signs her paycheck."

"Dad, things will work out."

"I'm beginning to wonder."

"I'll tell you if I think it's hopeless. I'm still hoping I can work things out with her." She followed him into the far greenhouse. "Where are these hybrids?"

They had worked together for about an hour. Jeff beamed with pride as his youngest daughter coached him on some of the new techniques she'd learned in school.

"I'm thinking of trying to graft a pink dogwood to a white dogwood. I don't usually like the grafted trees. You have the genetics of two trees in one trunk. They produce the long suckers that reach to the sun and drain the energy away from the blooms. But I think it would be pretty and fun to try." She looked up at her dad. "What are you smiling at?"

"You. I hope you know how proud I am of you." He leaned to kiss her on the forehead just as the door to the greenhouse opened. His brother Brian came in with David right behind him.

"Hey, David, Brian, what brings you two all the way out here?" Brian looked slightly less depressed than he had been, but only slightly. David looked hopeful.

"Victoria said you were out here." Brian said.

"Is Vic here today? She hasn't come in for a while. So, what's up?" Jeff looked from Brian to David.

"I don't know," David said. "Dad just said he wanted to talk to you about something. He wanted me to come along."

"What's up, Brian?" Jeff hoped that whatever it was would be good news, not more bad.

"Well, you know, I've been kind of floundering lately. I mean I don't know what to do now that Charlotte's gone." He pinched the bridge of his nose and closed his eyes. Everyone in the room tensed. "I..." He straightened his shoulders and looked up. The crisis seemed to have passed. "I went into one of those wild bird places the other day. I was thinking maybe a bird feeder outside my apartment window would help. Maybe it would add some life to my days."

"Sounds like a great idea, Dad." David put his hand on his father's back.

"I got to thinking about it. You know, Jeff, most nurseries have a wild bird section. Why don't we?"

It was the first time Jeff had heard Brian take any ownership of the family business. "I've just never been interested in that end of the business. We do alright without it. Why?"

"I was thinking I might like to clear a corner of the place and put in a wild bird section. I don't think it would hurt us or anything."

Jeff was silent. He was surprised that Brian would want to spend so much time in the nursery since he hated the smell of dirt. He wasn't going to say that. His brother's mental health had been so shaky lately. He glanced at Evelyn hoping she wouldn't say anything either. She opened her mouth to speak and he tensed.

"I think that's a great idea, Uncle Brian. I've thought of that myself." She looked at her father and frowned at the relief on his face. I'm not that clumsy, she thought. "Don't you think that's a great idea?"

"You don't have to give me an answer right now. Just think about it." Brian turned to leave.

"Wait a minute, Uncle Brian." Evelyn went to him and stood on her toes to kiss his cheek. He still had to lean down to her. "I'll help you find a corner." She glanced at her father. He didn't say anything as Brian left the room.

"Don't you even think of saying no," David said.

"That's right, Dad. Uncle Brian needs us right now. Besides, it's a good idea."

"I wasn't going to say no. I was just surprised. That's the first time he's said more than two words to me in months."

*

Evelyn left the greenhouse feeling excited about life. It was the first time she'd felt that way for a while. Things had been more difficult than she'd expected when she got home from school. But with the landscaping job and the corporate business she couldn't wait to get started on, she was feeling pretty good. Now with her uncle's new wild bird section, she wondered if she was getting in over her head. She hoped so. She loved being in over her head. Hadn't she always carried a double load at school? Most people didn't finish undergrad and masters in five years. She had.

Her dad had gone home about an hour before, leaving her to finish up in the greenhouse. She was going to get her sketch pad and notebook and head out to the Martin's house. She had just a few more notes to make before she could finalize the plans. The meeting with them was set for the following week. She'd be ready. Oh yes, she'd be ready.

"Just real proud of yourself, aren't you? Rose through the ranks pretty quickly." Darcy stood at the door to her office with her arms crossed. "With all that you're doing now, you don't have time to give to us lowly employees. It must be nice to be the owner's daughter."

"I'm not the owner's daughter, Darcy. I'm one of the owners. Now if you'll excuse me." She squeezed around her and through the door. "I don't have time for this right now. I have work to do."

She would not let the bitch ruin her mood. She was determined. She walked out of the office suite into the shop just in time to see Alice going up the steps deep in conversation with Jamie Parnell. She cringed inside. What's going on there? She wondered. Hadn't Alice been distant before her mother's accident? No. She wouldn't think like that. He was probably here to see David. She went on to her car and on to her work. But she was uncomfortable. She was definitely uncomfortable.

Chapter 7

Alice got out of her car and headed for the nursery. It was lunch time. She didn't want to interrupt the lunch rush at the café so she headed for the back stairs.

"Alice." She heard her name called very quietly and looked over her shoulder. Jamie stood next to the front steps with his finger pressed to his lips. She smiled and went to him.

"What's up?"

"I was hoping to avoid Ev. I know she's here because her car is in the parking lot. I wanted to talk to you."

"Well, I don't know if you can avoid her. She does work here. You could have called me."

"I wanted to talk to Uncle David, too. I figured this was the best place to get you both together. I know you told him about my problem. Dad talked to him after I talked to the family. He admitted that he already knew."

"Well, at least he waited until after you talked to your family. I guess he didn't betray my trust," she murmured.

"What?"

She looked up at Jamie's puzzled expression. "Never mind. I'll go look inside to see if she's around. I want to go up the back stairs to avoid busting into the lunch rush." She went to the door, stepped inside for a minute, then opened the door and motioned Jamie to follow her.

"So, what's the big news? I have to admit I talked to your friend Helen. She mistook me for Ev and told me you had big news before I had time to correct her."

"The two of you look very similar at a glance."

"Most people think we're identical." She laughed. "Even I think we're identical with my hair cut short. Why can you always tell us apart?"

"You just don't look that much alike to me."

They reached the top of the stairs and Jamie held the door open for her. They went through the smaller dining area and into the office.

"Maybe it's because you're in love with Ev."

"Maybe."

"So ..." Alice put her bag on her desk. "You are still in love with her."

Jamie shrugged his shoulders. "You tricked me into saying that."

"Yes, I did, but it's the truth, isn't it?"

"I guess I'll always be in love with her." His shoulders seemed to sag. He sat down on the love seat in the office. Alice sat at her desk.

David appeared in the doorway. "I saw you come in. What's up Jamie?"

"I wanted to talk to you and Alice. I have some good news."

"Great." Alice sat forward. She was glad for the interruption. Jamie had looked so defeated. She probably shouldn't have tricked him into his admission of love. But now that she was sure, she would find a way to get them back together.

"I got promoted to instructor at the school. I'm still staff but I'm not an assistant anymore. That means more money."

"That's great, son." David put his hand on Jamie's shoulder and squeezed. "That should help with the rescue project."

"It will help but it's still just a drop in the bucket. That's why I wanted to talk to you, Uncle David. I was wondering if you would help me write the prospectus thing. I'm going to try again for a small business loan."

"Of course, I will. I wish you'd asked me in the first place."

"I was too proud." Again, Jamie's face fell. "I guess I'm learning not to be proud."

"Hey, kid." David sat down at his desk. "You have a lot to be proud of. You're a fantastic tennis player. You teach it well. You had excellent grades in school. But there isn't anything wrong with asking for help."

"I guess not but this mess I've gotten myself into has been a very humbling experience."

"We all need to be humbled from time to time."

"Jamie," Alice said. "Is there some way I could help you in the meantime? I could do a couple of feedings or something like that."

"I've got that pretty well under control. I have some volunteers, vet techs and kennel people that help me out on that. I was wondering if maybe you would talk to your dad for me. Find out what's involved in the rescue program for the horses. You know, the cost of it, how much the rescue organization contributes. I'll need to know that stuff if I'm going to work up a budget for this prospectus thing."

"Why don't you talk to him yourself? You know what questions to ask. Why don't you come out there on Sunday? Ev and I are both off on Sundays. We could have dinner out there. Mom's been feeling kind of low. Maybe that would cheer her up. Like old times. You know how she used to tease you about your appetite."

He laughed. It made him look like his old self again. Alice could see why Evelyn loved him so much. Not only was he handsome, he was so genuine.

"I was always the last one up from the dinner table." He sobered again. "No thanks. I'd rather not. Your dad doesn't like me, and Ev and I aren't doing so good anymore."

"Okay, look..." It was a good idea but it didn't work, Alice thought. She changed tactics. "I'm off again on Friday. How about we go out there together? Dad won't bite. Besides, I don't think he dislikes you as much as you think he does."

Jamie drew his brows together in consideration.

"Come on. We can go riding. Dad has two rideable rescues. Although I think they're going to become members of the family."

"I never was much of a rider."

"You'll need to be able to if you're going to rescue. What if you get rideable rescues like Dad did. It'll give you a chance to see Sterling and Red. Haven't you missed them?"

"I have."

David stood up. "I think you should go, young James." He slapped Jamie on the back again. "I need to get back. We were starting to fill up the small room when I left. Let me know when you want to get started on the prospectus."

"Okay, I need to gather all the info first. I'll call you."

David went back out to the noisy café. Alice turned back to Jamie. "So, are we on for Friday?"

"I guess so." He stood up. "Alice, did you tell Ev about all this stuff?"

"No. I told you I wouldn't."

"Thanks. I know that's hard for you. You could tell her now if you want. Marisa will anyway. They seem to have become friends."

"I'll let your sister tell her then. Did you tell your family about my little trick?"

"No. I didn't see the point."

"I appreciate it. Maybe it could be our little secret. Ev gets kind of grouchy when I stick my nose into her business."

"You shouldn't do it then." He smiled, charming her again.

"I thought you said you could tell Ev and me apart. I'm the devious sister remember?"

*

Evelyn sat at her drafting table and added the finishing touches to her plans. She'd probably spent too much time on them. She'd have to get faster at this. Hopefully as time went by she'd pick up speed.

"How's it going?" Her father asked from the door.

"Oh ...! You startled me." She laughed.

"Sorry. The Martins should be here any minute. Are you sure you don't mind me sitting in on your meeting?"

"No. In fact, I could use the moral support."

"I don't know why. You're very well prepared." He looked over her shoulder at the plans she was working on.

"My mouth is as clumsy as the rest of me. You never know what I'll say." They laughed. He kissed the top of her head.

"What do you have planned for this afternoon?"

"Uncle Brian is coming to look around. We're going to choose a spot for his wild bird section."

"I think you're as excited as he is about this." Jeff went to the door to look out into the shop. "I was thinking of that back right corner. But the two of you decide. Any place is alright with me." He laughed. "Within reason, of course."

"I was thinking the back right corner too. Then I have to figure out how to approach Darcy about putting some people on clearing it out. I'll help, of course, but I can't do it alone."

"You don't have to help either. Didn't you say you had an appointment with a potential corporate customer."

"I'll fit it all in."

Jeff looked out into the nursery again. "The Martin's are here."

Evelyn took a deep breath and put her hand to her heart.

"Why are you so nervous, honey? I thought you and Mrs. Martin were friends."

"We get along pretty well. But I sure hope she likes my ideas. I'd hate to have to start all over."

"If you do, it'll be a chance for you to get used to it. It will happen in this business."

She stood up and went to the door to greet her customers. "You brought Bradley," she said as she greeted Ruth and Adam Martin. A child stood between them and extended his hand.

"Let's get the introductions straight from the beginning," he said as he shook both of their hands with a very firm grip.

"Be polite now, Bradley." Adam put his hand on the child's shoulder.

"I'm always polite."

Evelyn smiled as she saw Ruth roll her eyes.

"I prefer to be called Brad. Bradley is a fine name, but I hate the 'l-e-y. It sounds girly. God forbid you should call me Braddy. I don't know why people think they can put a 'y' on the end of a person's name just because it's a child. Do you like being called Evvy?" He looked so directly into Evelyn's eyes that she backed up a step.

"I don't think anyone has ever called me that."

"Would you like it if they did?

She thought about it for a minute. "No. I don't think I would."

"Then don't put a 'y' on the end of mine and we'll be fast friends."

"Fast friends." Evelyn resisted the urge to chuckle. "Let's go across the shop to the break room. There will be more room there. I hope you don't mind if Dad sits in."

"No of course not." Adam shook Jeff's hand. "I'm Adam Martin and this is ... Well you've met Bradley. He allows us to call him that." He smiled. "I believe you've met my wife Ruth."

"Yes, I have." Jeff directed them toward the break room and followed them in.

Evelyn rolled the plans out on the table and explained them. Her voice shook at first then smoothed out as she went along. She glanced at her father a couple of times and was pleased to see a smile on his face. She finished her explanation and stopped. Her mouth was a little dry so she went to the water cooler.

"Would you like some?" She asked.

"No thank you." All three of the Martins were looking at the plans. Their faces didn't reveal their thoughts. They asked a couple of questions. Evelyn's heart was pounding. She hoped her face wasn't red. She had a feeling it was.

"Can we take these plans home to study them?" Bradley asked. "I believe I have a few improvements to suggest. Not that they're bad." He smiled at Evelyn. "They just need a little polish." The child rolled up the plans and put them under his arm. He was big for four years old, but the long thick roll of plans looked like it was going to pull him over sideways. Again, Evelyn stifled the urge to laugh. She looked at her father. He was doing the same.

"I haven't had them copied yet. I could bring you a copy this afternoon," Evelyn said.

"I can have them copied and run them by on my way home. I'm getting ready to leave now anyway." Jeff put his hand out to Bradley for the plans.

"That would be great," Ruth said. "We'll see you in a little while then." She turned to Evelyn and smiled. "I'll call you."

Evelyn smiled broadly until she heard the front door to the shop close. She didn't feel like laughing anymore. She turned and buried her face in her father's chest. She gulped at the lump in her throat. The tears came anyway.

"I know, baby. You wanted them to love your plans right away." He held her at arm's length and kissed her forehead. "But hey, they didn't say they didn't like the them."

"I know." She rubbed her eyes with the back of her hand. She felt like a small child again. "I don't even know how they felt. Bradley, I mean Brad, did all the talking. What if they hated them?"

"It's a tough lesson to learn but trust me. I've had a lot worse happen. If you stay in this business you will too."

"But my first job. That's not a good sign."

"For what it's worth, I thought you handled yourself beautifully. I was so proud of my little girl."

"It's worth a lot, Dad."

"Good. Well I'd better get going if I'm going to get those plans copied. I don't like to leave your mom for too long. She's having a good day today but you never know how long it'll last."

"Give her a kiss for me. Tell her I love her."

*

Evelyn opened the door to her apartment. She let out a yelp when Sugar pounced on her shoulder. "Where did you come from? Oh, there." She shrugged, detached the little cat's claws from her sweater and assessed the damage. There were scattered books and pictures all over the floor. "I can't believe someone as small as you can do this much damage." He must have climbed up the book shelf and knocked anything in his way onto the floor.

"I'm just glad I have carpet," she said. "Otherwise this snow globe would be broken."

She picked up the mess and went to the kitchen to fill Sugar's food bowl.

"I guess you're hungry. I need to leave you a little more food," she said to the kitten as he dug into his food. "After all you're a growing boy." She stroked his back. He arched up and began to purr without interrupting his meal.

She went into the bedroom and took off her clothes to take a shower. Working in the dirt all day long required a shower in the evening. While she lathered herself, she tried to identify the melancholy feeling she'd had all day. Was she angry about something? Was she sad about something? Lonely. That's it. I'm lonely.

She missed Jamie but she'd gotten used to that. After all, he hadn't wanted anything to do with her for a long time. Alice was a different matter. Whenever she'd been in town from school she and Alice had been inseparable. Since she'd been home they'd spent as much time together as their schedules allowed. But lately it almost seemed like Alice was avoiding her.

She got out of the shower and dried herself off. She dressed and went to the living room to sit down and watch some TV. Sugar jumped into her lap, curled up and began to purr.

"What would I do without you, kid? Nobody else wants to spend time with me." She looked at the sliding glass door to her balcony and saw the sign for the café. "Alice is probably pretty busy right now." She stroked the warm, sleepy kitten. "I haven't had dinner. Maybe I'll go over. I could sit at the bar." She picked up Sugar and kissed him. "I'll be back soon."

She went up the back stairs of the café and through to the kitchen. "Hey, Jake." The night chef nodded at her.

"Alice is in the office," he said. "We're a little slow tonight. I'm not worried but you know how she is."

"I'll look in on my way to the bar. I'm here for dinner."

"There's plenty. The special's great."

"Dish me up some. I'll be out in a minute."

She tapped on the door before she opened it. Alice sat at the desk. She was on the phone and motioned Evelyn into the room.

"I have to go. My sister's here." She hung up the phone. Something about the way she said it made Evelyn suspicious.

"I guess that wasn't a customer. You didn't have to hang up so fast."

"It was a vender." Her eyes shifted.

"At this time of night?"

"The restaurant business never stops. So, what's up?"

"I came to have dinner. I didn't feel like cooking." She looked around the office. "And I figured you couldn't avoid me here."

"What are you talking about? Why would I avoid you?" Alice stood and started to the door. "I need to go on out. I'm hostessing tonight."

"You're avoiding me again. So, answer your own question. Why would you avoid me?"

"Ev, you know I'd never avoid you. I've just been busy. Come on." She continued through the door. "Let's go out and get you some dinner. We're a little slow tonight. I'll sit at the bar with you awhile."

"Well, okay."

Business picked up after a few minutes and Alice had to go back to work. Why did she look relieved?

*

"I have to run by the Martin's house today," Evelyn told Darcy on Thursday morning. "Ruth wanted to go over the plans with me. I'll be back in as soon as I get finished."

"When do you think that will be? We have two shipments coming in. We're short people since the part time kids went back to school. I know it's beneath you but I need some help."

Evelyn closed her eyes and counted to ten. This hostility was getting very old. "I can't give you a time. It depends on how long it takes. I'll get back as soon as I can."

"I guess it depends on how many changes she wants to make. Not feeling so high and mighty since your first assignment didn't turn out so great, huh?"

"No. I'm very humbled." Evelyn picked up her purse and notebook and left before Darcy could be any nastier.

Evelyn stood outside of the Martin's door and steadied her nerves. What if they didn't like them at all. What if ... "No," she said and rang the doorbell.

Ruth opened the door. "Come in, Evelyn." She ushered her into the living room. "Let's go into the dining room. Bradley is in there looking at the plans. That's pretty much what he's been doing since we left Landrum's." She laughed.

"I hope it didn't interfere with his homework." Evelyn sat down in a chair at the table next to Bradley.

"Homework is not a problem for me," he said. "Now, I have a few concerns."

"I hope the plans weren't hard to understand."

"No, they're very clear. We like them very much." Ruth poured two cups of coffee from a service on a buffet and put one down in front of Evelyn. She stood beside Evelyn's chair to look at the papers. "I think it's going to be beautiful. I'm sorry if we gave you the impression we didn't like the plans.

"No, not at all." Evelyn released a breath she hadn't realized she was holding and sipped her coffee. "What were your concerns, Brad?"

"This ledge here where you have the Trumpet vine." He pointed to the plans. Evelyn looked at his small hand and smiled. Cute, she thought. "I went up yesterday afternoon. I believe the angle is wrong. The roots won't hold. The gravitational pull will be too great. Of course, that could be remedied by digging back into the rock, but I wouldn't want to compromise the stability of the hill."

"You went up," Evelyn said. "I thought you were too smart to climb the wall."

"I'm too smart to climb the wall and get into the traffic on the highway. Scaling the rock face isn't stupid. Don't worry I used my rock climbing equipment."

"Oh. I'm glad to hear that." He turned back to the plans and Evelyn looked at Ruth. She smiled and shrugged her shoulders.

"I found a spot that I think will be better." He pointed to a spot slightly higher on the hill. "It has a natural crevice. In fact, when I was up there I pulled a couple of young sweet gum trees out. There's already soil there. I think the vine would look great cascading over the side of the ledge."

"Yes, I guess it would. That's higher than I had planned to go, but I suppose the crew can get to it. Maybe they could come in from the top."

"Not a problem. I can do it."

"Brad." Evelyn couldn't help but laugh. "Why pay a landscape crew if you're going to do the work."

"Oh, don't worry. They'll earn their pay. I plan to oversee the whole project."

"What about school?"

"I'm home schooled, remember? We'll work out the scheduling."

Bradley had a couple of other concerns, nothing that couldn't be worked out. Evelyn was even able to convince him that her way was better once.

"Do you have anything to add?" Evelyn asked Ruth when it looked like Bradley was finished.

"There's just one thing."

"Mom." Bradley crossed his arms and looked at his mother. "We've discussed this."

"Bradley, your father will live here too. In fact, he's paying for all of this. He has a right to his input."

Evelyn braced herself.

"Adam likes running water. He grew up next to a river. He says it's soothing. We looked and looked for property that had running water but we couldn't afford any of the places we saw. I was wondering if there was any place we could put in a fountain. Personally, I have seen some tacky fountains. We've quarreled about this. You can see how Bradley feels about it. But it's important to Adam. So, it's important to me."

Was that all, Evelyn breathed a sigh of relief. "Have you seen the fountain display at the shop? Do any of those appeal to you."

"Sorry. No."

"Mom." Evelyn looked back at Bradley. Was his voice quivering. "You know why I don't want a fountain." He sniffed and wiped his face as tears began to spill onto his cheeks. "Please don't put one in."

"Honey, we'll talk about this later. Go up to your room. Let me finish talking to Evelyn. I'll come up when we're done."

"I hate you!" Bradley ran toward the stairway. "I hate Dad, too. You're both mean."

"Wow." Evelyn stared after him.

"He is only a child after all," Ruth said. "The transitions are scary though, aren't they?"

"Why doesn't he want a fountain."

"He's afraid it will make him pee in his bed. He has a slight bed wetting problem." She talked in undertones. "We've explained that we'll turn the fountain off at night and whenever we're not out there. But he says just knowing it's there will cause a problem. His little brain just works too hard."

"I see what you mean about higher intelligence being as much of a challenge as anything else. Maybe it would be better not to put in a fountain."

"No. With a child like Bradley it's important to impress on him that he isn't more important than other people just because he's smarter. He also has to learn to deal with stress and anxiety. There will be a lot of it as active as his brain is."

"Well then, I have some resources for fountains. I think I can find one that you and Adam can agree on, maybe even one Brad can agree on. Let's go out back and have a look." She glanced back at the stairway. "Will he be alright? Do you need to go up first?"

"No. Let him think about it for a while."

They spent a few minutes in the back yard. Evelyn left feeling excited about the ideas swimming around in her head. She was going to come up with the perfect solution. Ruth had said that she and Adam would come in to sign the contract the following day.

She started back to work then changed her mind. She didn't want to deal with any more hostility today. She was feeling too good. Darcy and the loading dock would have to be dealt with tomorrow. She grimaced. She decided to go out to see her parents and pulled the car onto the highway. That way she could tell her dad her good news and check on her mom at the same time.

She was surprised to see Alice's car in the driveway. Alice had Fridays off but with her nights at the café she usually wasn't up and moving this early in the morning.

"Hey, Dad," she called as he came out of the barn with a horse she hadn't seen before. "A new rescue?"

"Yeah, this is Sweetie. She's an old lady with shin splints. I was hoping she would get along with Elmo. He's a little lonely since Doris died."

"So, how's it going?"

"They're doing okay. They aren't in love but I think they'll be okay. They seem to be warming up to each other."

"Good. I didn't expect to see Alice's car here. Where is she?"

"She and James, Jr. are up at the barn looking at Roan and Dapple. Alice wants to go for a ride. James, Jr. didn't look too enthusiastic. I'm sure he'd appreciate it if you went up there. Not having enough horses to go around would be a good excuse not to ride."

He'd always called Jamie James, Jr. And there was always a note of disapproval on the words. He'd had a hard time with the age difference.

Evelyn looked in the direction of the barn just as Alice and Jamie rode out and up the hill. They didn't look in the direction of the house so they didn't see her. She couldn't help but chuckle at Jamie's awkward seat but inside she had a very uncomfortable feeling.

"I guess it's too late." Jeff laughed. "Poor James, Jr. I hope he doesn't take too bad a spill."

"So, they came out here to ride. I'm surprised Alice is up at this time of day."

"I was too. Apparently, James has to go to work this afternoon. He wants to talk to me about something. Are you two seeing each other again? He's not about to ask for your hand, is he?"

"No. You don't have to worry about that." She turned and put her arms around her father's waist. He hugged her back.

"Is everything alright, honey? Is everything alright between you and Alice? I haven't seen the two of you together lately."

"Everything is fine. We're just busy with our separate lives," she said. How did Alice's separate life involve Jamie? That was the question. "I've got good news. I came out to tell you in person."

"What is it?"

"The Martins are coming in to sign the contract tomorrow. Brad had a number of things to discuss with me. The only problem Ruth and Adam had with the plans was that Adam wants a fountain and Ruth doesn't. She thinks they're tacky."

"Has she seen our display?"

"Yeah, she doesn't like any of them. But it's important to Adam so she's asked me to try to design one that won't be tacky. I was thinking about using the natural look of that rocky cliff in the back yard. I'll have to work on it. I think some sort of a waterfall with a pool at the bottom. I just don't know how we'd run the tubing behind the rocks."

"Sounds great! I've built a few water falls using the natural landscape. Would you like me to take a look with you? If you'd rather do it yourself just say so."

She smiled up at him. "I would really appreciate your help. One of the reasons I've always wanted to do this is so we could work together."

"Good. Arrange a time with Ruth when we can go out there. Let me know. I'm pretty open these days." He glanced at the house. Evelyn caught a fleeting expression of anxiety.

"How's Mom?"

"Up and down." Jeff pulled his brows together. "I'm just taking it a day at a time. There doesn't seem to be anything I can do."

"No, I don't think there is. I'll just go in and say hello. Then I need to go. I'm going to spend the evening with my sketch pad. I have some ideas I want to get down before I forget them."

*

Evelyn threw herself into her work the next day. She didn't want to think what she was thinking about Alice and Jamie. That was the second time she'd seen them together. What was going on? It was bad enough that Jamie didn't want her anymore. She just wouldn't be able to stand it if he turned to Alice.

Okay. It didn't matter how hard she worked. She couldn't stop thinking about it. It would be awful if this caused a rift between her and her twin. But it would be awful to see them together when she loved him so much. What if they got married? What if it's the real thing? What if they're really in love? Shouldn't she be happy for them? Was she that small that she couldn't be happy that her sister had found love? Even if it was with Jamie?

"Yes," she said out loud. "I'm that small!"

"Look." Darcy turned with her hands on her hips. "I'm not that much bigger than you and I'm lifting this stuff."

"I didn't mean I was too small to do this work, Darcy. I was just thinking out loud about something not pertaining to this job."

"Well, get back to work and try not to trip over your feet." She turned her back to walk away.

Evelyn reached for a bag of potting soil. The bag was broken and her hand sunk into the soil. She grabbed a handful of dirt and hurled it at Darcy's back.

"You little bitch!" Darcy turned and reached into the bag. She smeared a handful of dirt on both of Evelyn's cheeks.

"I'm a bitch? I only bounced a little off your back." She reached back into the bag and pulled out more soil. Reaching up she rubbed it into Darcy's hair.

They reached for the bag at the same time. The hole wasn't big enough so they both took hold of the bag and ripped. They plunged in and came up with two handfuls each. Darcy scrubbed hers into Evelyn's hair while Evelyn smeared it down the front of Darcy's t-shirt.

They both went for the bag again and pulled it off the back of the truck. This knocked both of them onto the dock. Evelyn rolled out from under the bag and stood up grabbing for another handful of dirt.

Darcy raised herself up on her elbows but couldn't scramble to her feet as fast as the younger woman.

Evelyn was poised to pummel her with soil when the humor of the situation hit her. She burst into laughter, dropped the soil, and extended her hand to Darcy. Darcy's expression went from sour to a reluctant smile then laughter. She took the extended hand and pulled herself up. They both sat on the back of the truck and laughed. The driver of the truck looked around reluctantly. They broke into another round of laughter.

"Are you two finished?" He smiled. "I was hoping I wasn't going to have to break it up. I've got another stop to make and I didn't want to be covered with dirt."

"We're finished," Evelyn said. "And we're finished unloading. That was the last bag. Thanks, Jack. We'll see you next time." They both got up and walked toward the greenhouse to clean up.

"Darcy," Evelyn said as she wiped her face with a cloth. "We've got to work this thing out. I remember when Alice and I were kids I could tell you didn't think Dad should bring us here as much as he did. But that was because we were always getting in the way. What's the problem now? I'm not in the way."

The laughter she'd seen on Darcy's face was gone. It had been replaced by the sour disapproving look she'd seen so much more often.

"What is it, Darcy?"

"I know you're after my job." She scowled. "And I know if you want it, I'm out of luck. Your dad will give you anything you want. I've worked here too long and too hard to be replaced by some inexperienced little spoiled brat."

Evelyn stood silent for a minute. She was determined not to respond to the hostility. She could see now that it was fueled by fear. Darcy had devoted her life to this place.

"Darcy, how long have you worked with Dad?"

"Twenty-three years. I've put my whole self into this place. I'm a long way from retirement. I don't want to start over somewhere else." The anger in her voice was being slowly replaced by something else. What was it? Desperation?

"Darcy." Evelyn sat down on a stool. "You know him better than that. He's a loyal person. He appreciates your hard work."

"I know he does." She sounded sad now. "And he wouldn't fire me. He'd just find me some menial thing to do. He probably wouldn't even lower my salary." She looked up. Were those tears in her eyes? "Evelyn." It was the first time she'd called her by her name since she'd been back. "You know he'll do anything for you. Maybe you're not a brat. I guess I shouldn't have said that. But you have to admit you are spoiled. So is your sister."

Evelyn smiled. "Yes, I am spoiled. I'll admit it. He would probably give me your job if I asked for it. And you're right. He would find you something else to do." She stood and went to the sink to rinse out the cloth. "The thing is. I don't want your job." She turned and looked at Darcy again. "I want his."

A slow smile spread over Darcy's features.

"What's going on here?" Jeff stood in the doorway. "The loading dock is a mess." He looked them both up and down. "And look at the two of you."

They looked at each other and broke into laughter again.

*

Jamie entered the cafeteria and frowned. His sister Marisa was sitting in the corner with her head so close to Mike's they were practically necking. He went to the table and sat down.

"Will the two of you cut it out. You're in public."

"We weren't doing anything but talking." Marisa pulled back and smiled.

"I don't know how you can talk with your lips that close together."

Mike laughed and stood up. "You're going to have to get used to it, Jamie."

"Well, I'd appreciate it if you'd save your affections for the privacy of your own house."

"You're out of luck there." He slapped Jamie on the shoulder and leaned down to kiss Marisa. "I've got to go. I have a class. It was nice to see you, sweetie. What a nice surprise."

Marisa smiled at Mike's back as he walked away. Then she turned to Jamie.

"I didn't actually come over here to see him. I came to see you."

"Yeah, why?"

"Evelyn is worried that you and Alice have a thing going."

"What! That's ridiculous! She's like my sister."

"It may seem that way to you, but Alice is not your sister." She sat back and looked around the room. "Ev called and asked me to have lunch with her today. I told her I already had a date with Mike. I wanted to talk to you and find out what you want me to tell her. I don't want to embarrass you but it'll be hard not to tell her what's going on."

Jamie sighed. "Tell her. Maybe it'll make her see that she doesn't need a loser like me."

"What are you talking about. You're not a loser. In fact, on the tennis court you're a winner. You've got a position at the school. Just because you couldn't get your masters doesn't make you a loser. Education isn't everything."

"Says my sister who is following in my older sister's footsteps and going to medical school. I can't even get a master's in Physical Education."

"Big deal."

"Besides, I couldn't support a family on what I make here, and look at the mess I'm in with the rescue."

"I can't believe you didn't tell us about that. We all thought you were in trouble." She reached across the table and put her hand on his arm. "Or that you'd gone crazy."

"I am in trouble and I have gone crazy."

"No, you haven't. With the loan David is going to help you get the rescue will do great. I know it'll be non-profit but you'll be able to take a salary. That'll help. Jamie, Evelyn loves you."

"She shouldn't."

"She does."

He looked down at his hands. He could feel his sister's eyes on him. She was studying his face.

"What?" He finally looked up.

"Maybe you are stupid."

"Thanks. I needed that."

"You have this fantastic woman in love with you and you're in love with her. Are you really going to let money get in the way?"

"It's more than money."

"What is it then?"

"She deserves someone better, someone who can support her, someone with more potential."

"She can support herself. She can even support you. Don't tell me you're stuck in the past and don't like the idea of being supported by your wife."

Jamie looked up. His eyes flashed with anger. "She is not my wife. She never will be. And, no, I don't want a wife to support me."

Anger is a good thing, Marisa thought. It was the first time she'd seen anything but defeat in his eyes for a long time. She studied him for another minute.

"What?" He said again.

"Maybe you're not stupid. Maybe you're just being a martyr."

"How do you get martyr?"

"Sacrificing your true love on principal. You're a martyr and you're stupid. I guess I'll tell Evelyn the whole story. You're right. She needs to know what a loser you are." She stood up and stormed out of the cafeteria.

He watched her, smiling despite her assault. His baby sister was a spitfire. He felt a little bad for Mike.

Chapter 8

"Manda!" Jeff stood at the door to their bedroom. "It's almost noon. Please get up. It's a beautiful day. Let's go for a walk."

"Leave me alone, Jeff. I don't want to get up. I don't ever want to get up again."

"Manda." He sat beside her on the bed and pulled the sheet off her head. "You have to snap out of this. What's wrong? Talk to me."

She pulled the sheet back up over her head. "There is just no place in this world for me anymore. I've done all I was here to do. It's time for me to go. I pray every day that God will take me away. I don't know why He won't."

"I hate it when you talk like that."

"Don't ask then."

"Okay! Stay in the damn bed!" He stood and stormed to the door. He stopped with his hand on the knob and turned. "I never knew you were a coward, Manda. I always thought you had a lot of courage. You're just afraid. That's all. At this point in our lives things aren't as well defined as they've been in the past. We have to define our lives ourselves. There's no more step by step. You're just too much of a coward to even try." He slammed the door behind him as he left.

He stormed down the steps and out of the front door. The dogs fell in beside him as he went to the gate of the larger pasture. It had been a while since he'd walked the fence line to check for any damage. He'd just do it himself. It had always been something he and Amanda did together. Well, he'd just do it himself from now on. He wasn't finished with this life. He still had things to do.

Before he'd gone more than a couple hundred feet a car turned into the driveway and backfired. He jumped and looked up.

"Whoa, what a wreck," he said to himself as it came down the drive. He watched as it pulled to a stop beside the fence. It backfired again, then groaned as the motor shuttered to a stop.

James Jr. stepped out from the behind the wheel and started toward him.

"I can't believe that thing made it all the way out here." Jeff leaned his elbows on the fence.

"It's not as bad as it looks." Jamie smiled sheepishly. "It's not as bad as it sounds either."

"So," Jeff said. "Was there something you wanted to talk to me about?"

"Yes sir." He looked around uncomfortably. "I was hoping to get a look at Sterling and Red. They were quite a project for me, being feral and all. I kind of miss them at the shelter."

"Is that what you chanced driving that thing out here for, just to see the barn cats?"

"Well, no, I was wondering if you'd come to my place and have a look. Maybe help me figure out where to put the barn and stuff. I've never done much with horses."

"I'm not exactly an expert, James."

"No, but you have more experience than anyone else I know. Maybe you could introduce me to your horse rescue group. It would be good for me to learn about it before I open mine. If I get the loan that is."

"David tells me you'll get the loan. He'll co-sign with you if it's necessary."

"I wouldn't let him do that, sir. That wouldn't be right. I got myself into this mess. I'll get myself out. I'll accept his help with the prospectus thing, but that's all."

"You sound a little more hopeful than you did the other day when we talked."

"Alice has helped me with that. You can't feel hopeless around Alice." He smiled sheepishly again. "She just won't have it."

Jeff stepped back from the fence and walked along toward the gate. Jamie walked on the other side.

"You're not getting involved with Alice now are you, Jamie?" Jeff could hear the growl in his own voice. "That would cause a problem between them. I won't help you with anything if you cause a problem between my girls."

"Oh no, sir." Jamie turned and looked at him earnestly. "Alice and I are friends, really good friends and that's important. But I'll never love any woman but Evelyn. Never!" Jamie turned and shuffled his feet but not before Jeff saw the blush rising up his neck to his face.

"So, you're still in love with her?"

"Yes, sir. You and Alice are a lot alike. She tricked me into admitting that too." He laughed and looked down at his feet. "I'll leave her alone though, sir. You don't have to worry. You never liked us going out and you were right. She doesn't need a loser like me."

Jeff studied the young man in front of him. He was a good-looking kid and pretty smart as long as he didn't have to take an English exam. That had nothing to do with his intelligence, though. He'd had some pretty substantial learning problems. James was squirming under his scrutiny.

"You're right! She doesn't need a loser like you!"

James looked up at him with the closest thing he'd ever seen to fire in his eyes. There was still some fight in the kid. He went through the gate and put his arm across Jamie's shoulders.

"Look, James. I wasn't happy at first when the two of you started dating. After all, she was only seventeen. You were into your twenties."

"Twenty-three."

"But you kept promising me that you wouldn't take advantage of her innocence." He tried to ignore the fresh blush on Jamie's face. "After a while I realized I was more worried about her taking advantage of your innocence." Now Jamie was a deep red and Jeff changed the subject. The kid's expression revealed a little bit more than he wanted to know.

They went to the barn where the rescued horses were in hopes of finding the cats there. They looked at each horse. Jamie helped him lead each of them out of the stall. Jeff showed him how to brush them and check their hoofs. Then they turned them out into the pasture to graze.

"Well, I guess the cats are at the other barn. They're great mousers. We haven't had a problem since they came."

"It was a perfect situation for them. They could never have been indoor cats. I'm not even sure they could have adjusted to living in the city."

They crossed the driveway and went into the barn where the new rescue horse and Elmo lived. Amanda sat on a bale of hay holding the silver tabby in her lap. Jeff stopped short.

"Hey, Mrs. Landrum." Jamie walked over to her to pet the cat. "Isn't she a great cat? Where's Orange? I mean Red."

Amanda cleared her throat. "He was right here a minute ago. She sure is happy to see you." The cat in her lap purred so loudly Jeff could hear it across the barn.

"She seems to like you a lot too." Jamie smiled at her. She smiled back. Jeff stifled a gasp.

Jamie squatted to pet the orange cat that had joined them, purring just as loudly. "You must spend a lot of time with them."

"No." She stood and put the cat down. They both rubbed on Jamie's legs. "I really haven't seen them since they came. I just wanted to check on Elmo. It was good to see you, Jamie." She headed toward the door.

Jamie looked at Jeff. The expression on his face said everything. Both Alice and Evelyn had mentioned their mother's depression. Jeff looked helpless. He reached for her arm as she passed him. She shrugged his hand off.

"Mrs. Landrum," Jamie said on impulse. She turned around. "You've done a lot of animal rescue, haven't you?"

"In the past, honey. That's behind me now." Jamie could almost hear the thought continue... 'just like everything else.'

"Mom says that when you can't do anymore, you teach. She gave up her hair salon because of the arthritis in her hands. She's teaching at a cosmetology school now."

"That's nice. I'm glad she's happy." Amanda smiled sadly and turned to leave.

"I was thinking maybe you could teach me about rescue. I'm sure Mr. Landrum has told you about the mess I'm in. I can use all the help I can get."

"Oh, honey, I don't have the energy for that. Thanks for asking though. I'm flattered that you think I could help." She stood, looked out the door of the barn for a second then started out again.

"Mr. Landrum is coming out to see the place on ..." He looked at Jeff.

"Saturday. I think we decided on Saturday." Jeff looked at Jamie and smiled gratefully.

"That's right. Please come with him. I'd at least like for you to see the place. Even though it's a mess I'm proud of it. It took every penny I had just for the down payment."

Amanda took a deep breath but never turned around. "I guess I could do that." Then she turned. "I guess I'll see you Saturday."

"James, Jr. let me buy you a drink." When she'd left the barn, Jeff went over to where Jamie sat on the bale of hay that Amanda had left. "I haven't been able to get her to leave this place for weeks. Shoot, I haven't been able to get her to leave the house for weeks."

"I'd heard she was depressed." He stroked the cats that still rubbed on his legs. "She was always so dynamic. I was a little bit afraid of her. Now she looks like life has defeated her. I was feeling the same way a few weeks ago. It's awful."

"It's awful to see. Come into the house and have a cold beer."

"I'd like that, sir."

"James, do you think you could call me Jeff instead of Sir or Mr. Landrum. If we're going to work together on this project we should be on a first name basis."

"I'll try, Sir."

Just after Jamie pulled out of the driveway Alice pulled in.

"What was Jamie doing here?" She said when she went into the kitchen where her father was staring vacantly out the window. She tapped him on the shoulder. He jumped. "There's no mistaking that car." She laughed uneasily.

He seemed to tear his eyes away from the window. Then it took him a minute to focus on her.

"Dad, you were a thousand miles away."

"Yeah well, anyway, he was here to ask some questions about horses. He wants me to help him with the horse end of his rescue."

"When we talked to you a couple of weeks ago you didn't seem so excited about it. You sound like you're looking forward to it now."

"I am." He looked up and smiled. "That James, Jr. is a fine young man. Alice, what can we do to get him and Evelyn back together? They'll never be happy without each other."

Alice grinned broadly. "Well, I've got a plan."

"Uh oh." Jeff smiled and leaned forward. "Tell me about it."

*

"Marisa, over here." Alice called from the coffee house they were meeting in.

Marisa waved and crossed the room. She sat down on the other side of the corner booth. "What's this all about, Alice? Maybe I'm wrong but I've always had the feeling you didn't like me much. Why the sudden invitation for coffee?"

"Well." Alice bristled. "Let's just jump right in, why don't we?"

"See what I mean?"

"I would say you were the aggressor this time. In fact, you've always been the aggressor. You're such a brat."

"I guess it takes one to know one." Marisa scooted to the edge of the booth. "So, should we just get up and walk away right now or was there some reason why you asked me here despite our mutual hatred of each other?"

"Okay wait a minute." Alice looked down at the table and counted to four. People always said to count to ten, but her attention span wasn't that long. "We may not like each other but we both care about Jamie and Evelyn. Am I wrong?"

Marisa moved back into the booth. "No. You're not wrong about that. Why?"

"They're miserable without each other. Am I wrong?"

"You're not wrong about that either. So, are you suggesting that we can do anything about it? Because if you are, I should tell you I've already talked to Jamie about it until I'm blue in the face. He's a stubborn mule."

"He's admitted to me and to my dad that he still loves her."

"Really? I thought he was afraid of your dad."

"They're developing a relationship. I guess you know about his rescue plans by now."

"Yeah, he told the whole family. He came to dinner and made it like a big announcement. He's really embarrassed. I don't know how you can be embarrassed about something like that. It's so ..."

"Good. It's really a good thing to do."

"He thinks he's made a mess of it." Marisa smiled at the waitress. They both ordered coffee and scones. "I guess he has. Maybe if he'd asked for help in the first place he wouldn't be in this mess. Sometimes I don't know if he's proud or stupid."

Alice smiled. She'd had the same thought. "Have you seen his property, where he lives?" She could visualize the tiny cabin. She hoped he hadn't had to face that humiliation.

"No, have you?"

Apparently, Jamie hadn't told the family about her little prank. "Just briefly. It's kind of a mess at this point. If he gets that loan he'll do fine though. David says he'll get the loan. Anyway," she hurried on so Marisa wouldn't ask how she had seen the place. "That's not what I wanted to talk about. I think we need to put our heads together and figure out a way to get them back together again. Dad wants to help. There's a friend of Jamie's from school who's become friends with Evelyn who wants to help."

"You must mean Helen. You know I'm engaged to one of Jamie's colleagues. I'm a part of that crowd."

"Are you now?" Alice bristled at Marisa's tone.

"I wasn't being snooty, Alice. That's the problem with you. You're always reading things into what I say."

"Or maybe you're always saying things with an undertone. You've always thought you were superior."

Marisa moved over to the edge of the booth again. She opened her purse and pulled out her wallet.

"Wait a minute." Alice counted to four again. "We'll never accomplish anything if we can't keep from arguing. I really want them to get back together. They're good for each other."

Marisa edged back into the booth just as the waitress brought the coffee and scones. "Alright, what did you have in mind?"

"Evelyn is going to stay with Mom tomorrow while Dad comes into town to do some work. Our mother has been depressed lately."

"I'm sorry to hear that."

"Helen has agreed to meet me at the nursery at about 3:00. I was hoping you could be there too. Maybe if we all put our heads together we can think of something."

"You and your harebrained schemes. Jamie always talked about your harebrained schemes."

"Okay, forget it. I thought you could look past your turned-up nose long enough to help your brother. I guess I was wrong." This time Alice edged to the end of the booth.

"Wait a minute." Marisa sipped her coffee. "I'm in. I'll be there."

*

Jeff pulled into the gravel driveway off the dirt road that he had taken from the highway. "This is it," he said looking at the mailbox.

"I thought you said Jamie's address was 816. I only see 16." Amanda stretched her arms and yawned.

"Look a little closer. Right before the one there's a faint outline of an eight. One of the first things we're going to do is replace that mailbox. It's so rusted I'm sure his mail gets wet."

"Well, if you think this is it then go on down the driveway. Go slowly though. It looks a little rough."

Jeff turned the car down the drive and slowly made his way into the thick forest. "This place needs a lot of work."

"I don't know." Amanda opened her window and put her hand out into the cool air. "It's nice. It's so natural. I haven't been in a real forest for a long time."

Jeff glanced over at her. She hadn't said that much on the whole ride down. Maybe she was relaxing a little bit. "It sure is a long way out of town. I guess that's why he was able to get it so cheap."

"How do you know it was cheap?"

"He said he'd gotten a good deal on it."

They pulled into an opening and stopped. They both got out of the car and stared at the tiny building on the edge of the clearing. Both were silent for a full minute.

"You don't suppose that's where he lives?" Jeff spoke quietly.

"Surely not," Amanda whispered.

"Well, let's see." Jeff walked to the door of the tiny hut and knocked. The door opened and Jamie ducked out and straightened to his full height.

"Hey, Mr. Landrum." He smiled and shook Jeff's hand. "Mrs. Landrum, I'm so glad you came along." He bent to kiss her cheek.

"Jamie," Amanda said. "How tall are you?"

He smiled sheepishly and laughed. "Alice asked the same question. Yes. The house is shorter than me. I only use it to sleep so it doesn't matter."

"Honey, why don't you live in one of those mobile homes?" Amanda started walking toward the buildings.

"Those are the kennels," Jamie said as he hurried to catch up with her.

Jeff followed. He still hadn't said anything. He was stunned. He'd seen the kid's car. That was bad enough. These living conditions were unacceptable. Looks like the mailbox won't be the first thing we replace, he thought.

"Jamie," Amanda said as they stepped into the first building. "You know, this place is not bad." She walked down the narrow path between the kennels. "It doesn't smell bad in here like I thought it would. How do you keep it so clean with this many dogs in here?" She stopped at the end cage and looked in at the dog inside of it.

"I work pretty late sometimes. But the dogs are pretty good about going when they get out in the run. I rarely have to clean up poop in here. Dogs like clean living spaces."

"Tell me about this dog," she said.

Jamie went to stand beside her and look into the cage. "I call him Hampton. I found him in a dumpster on a street downtown named Hampton Street. He was rummaging."

"Hello, Hampton." Amanda stretched her hand toward the cage. "Is he friendly?"

"He's a little shy." The dog crawled toward the back of the cage. "I think he was a homeless dog. Kind of the dog equivalent of a homeless person."

"That's sad." Amanda stood and moved toward the door.

"Yes, ma'am. It is sad. That's why I want to do something about it. I mean I can't save them all. But I can save some of them. I've worked with Hampton a good bit. I think he'll make a good pet for someone if I can just get the word out. That's why I need you and Mr. Landrum to help me. You know about rescue."

"I don't know much about it. That's Jeff's area."

"That's not true, Manda," Jeff said startling himself with his voice. It was the first time he'd spoken since Jamie opened the door to his hut. "You've rescued dogs and cats all your life. At least ever since I've known you."

They stepped out of the trailer and headed toward the other mobile home.

"Now the cat room is a little stinkier. Cat's don't go outside. They use litter boxes. I've cleaned them today, but I can't seem to train them to poop all at the same time." He laughed as he reached for the door.

"No, cats aren't as cooperative as dogs." Jeff laughed and glanced at Amanda. She had chatted more since they'd been with Jamie today than she had in months. She was quiet now as they entered the cat room. The cages were stacked two high and weren't as big as the dog runs. But the place was clean and had only a faint smell of cat poop.

"Oswald." Jamie went directly to a cage at the back of the room. "I figured you'd poop as soon as I left." He looked at Amanda and Jeff. "He was the only one with a clean litter box about an hour ago. Let me take care of this." He pulled a scoop out of a plastic cabinet at the end of the building and turned to the pan.

"Do you mind if I let them move around a little bit?" He asked. "They all get along pretty well. I like to let them stretch their legs."

"Go ahead." Amanda moved to the first cage. "Can I help?"

"Sure. I don't let them all out at the same time usually, but I only have nine in here right now. We can handle the whole group." The big orange cat in the cage he was cleaning leapt to the ground.

Amanda opened two of the cages and Jeff opened two. Jamie finished what he was doing and opened the rest. The room was filled with exploring cats. They all moved from corner to corner. One zipped under the cages and batted at another from there. Two kittens found a toy ball in the corner and had a good game of bat the ball.

"Here." Jamie handed them both a stick with string and a feather on the end.

"Nothing better than a room full of cats is there, Manda?" Jeff looked up and sucked in his breath. She was smiling, but there were tears running down her cheeks.

"What's wrong, Mrs. Landrum? I didn't mean to upset you." Jamie went to her side.

"I'm not upset, Jamie. It's just that they're all so happy. Their lives are in limbo but they don't care." She looked over at the kittens that were rolling and pouncing on each other. She wiped her eyes with the back of her hand. "You said you only had nine cats in here. Did you have more at one time?"

"Yes, I can house twenty. I've only had that many once. But it fills up and empties out fast. Only Oswald has been here since I started. I think I'll keep him. He usually lives outside and sleeps with me."

"Where do the others go?"

"There's one pet store in town that lets me have an adoption day. The cats go pretty fast but the dogs are slow to move. I guess people think dogs are a bigger responsibility."

"Just one store?" Jeff asked.

"There are a lot of cat rescue groups. We vie for space. The shelter where I volunteer lets me bring some in there if they're not too full."

"How do you manage to volunteer anywhere when you have all this going on?"

"I like to stay busy."

They put the cats up and went back outside. Jamie showed them the pen where he let the dogs run. The chain link fence was probably ten feet high. It covered about half an acre.

"I plan to expand it when I get my loan. If I get it that is. I'm going to build a cat habitat too. I bought the chain link fencing yesterday. I'm planning to start on it tomorrow. The weather is cool but when you're working it feels good. It's nice to work outside on my weekends." He pointed to a freshly cleared piece of land. "I'm going to put it over there. It'll be small at first but I can expand."

"What about the stable?" Jeff asked. They walked up the hill toward the hut and stopped at the car.

"I haven't figured out where I'll put it yet." He headed toward the hut. "Would you guys like a drink. I have a little fridge in here I could get you a beer or a coke or something."

"I'd love a beer," Jeff said.

"I'd love one too." Jeff looked at Amanda, surprised.

"Sure." Jamie ducked into the hut. Jeff and Amanda sat down at a picnic table under an apple tree.

"You don't usually drink beer, Manda."

"It just appealed to me. I don't know why." Jamie came back out and handed her the can. She took a sip and laughed. "It's good. Why don't I drink beer, Jeff?"

"I don't know." He didn't want to say too much. She actually seemed to be enjoying herself. He looked back at

Jamie. "So, tell me, James Junior. When do you plan to change your living arrangements?"

"It's not a priority. We'll see after the loan."

"You're planning to do a lot with that loan. I hope it's a big one."

"Well, we'll see how far it goes."

"Do you take donations?"

"Whatever I can get."

"How about I donate a mobile home. I don't like to think of you getting stooped shoulders living in that hut. Actually, it looks more like a storage shed."

"Thanks, Mr. Landrum." Jamie shook his head. "I take donations for the animals, not charity for myself."

"It wouldn't be charity. It would be an investment. I plan for this place to take off. You can pay me back with interest."

"It would be charity."

"Really, James ..." Jeff started.

"Jeff." Amanda put her hand on his arm and shook her head.

"Okay, but you will at least let me donate a mail box. How are you going to read your mail if it's all wet?"

Jamie smiled and took a drink of his beer. "Okay. I guess I could take that much."

"I can donate time too. I could come out and help you work on the habitat tomorrow. You could help too, Manda. You said you liked the fresh air."

"I guess that would be okay." Amanda stood. "Maybe. I don't know." The sad expression was back on her face. Her shoulders slumped as she walked toward the car.

Jeff followed her with his eyes then looked back at Jamie.

"Mrs. Landrum." Jamie followed her to the car. He put his hand on her shoulder as she reached for the handle. "Would you do me a favor?"

She hesitated then turned around. "If I can."

"Wait here." He ducked into his hut again and reappeared with a tiny kitten in his hand.

"Ohhh..." She reached for the tiny creature.

"I think he must be feral. Either his mother dumped him or she lost him somehow. Probably she dumped him. Cats don't lose their kittens. Maybe she had too many. I was wondering if you'd take him for me, just until he's weaned."

"Oh no!" She tried to give him back to Jamie. He acted like he didn't notice.

"I fed him every four hours last night. I could do it all weekend, but I can't take him to work with me on Monday. The school doesn't let us bring pets. I doubt they'd make an exception for this little guy."

She tried to give him back again. Jamie still didn't take him. "I couldn't. I've never raised a bottle-fed kitten before. I didn't even bottle feed the girls." Jeff smiled at the slight blush on her face. "What if he dies?"

"Probably about half of the bottle-fed kittens die. But I think he should at least have a chance." This time he reached out to take the little cat. "I have a feeling this little guy won't die. He's pretty determined." He put the kitten back into her hands as it started to squirm and squeak. "At least would you hold him while I go get his bottle?"

Jeff moved closer to her and stretched his hands out. "Can I hold him for a minute, Manda."

She handed the tiny thing to him. Jamie came out of the hut with a tiny bottle.

"How old do you figure he is?" Jeff asked.

"No more than a couple of days." He took the wiggling squeaking thing back into his hands and pressed the tiny nipple of the bottle to its mouth. It turned its head and avoided the nipple. "You kind of have to push it into his mouth but once he gets it he takes off. See there he goes."

"Ohh..." Amanda covered her mouth as the tiny creature sucked hungrily at the bottle. Bubbles were floating to the surface of the liquid as the kitten sucked and swallowed.

"What are you feeding him?"

"It's called Kitten Milk Replacement, KMR. It's formulated especially for kittens."

"You mean they really make stuff like that?" Jeff laughed.

"They do. I guess this happens a lot. You want to feed him for a minute, Mrs. Landrum? I need to grab his blanket. It's a little chilly out here for him."

Amanda took the tiny thing from him without dislodging the bottle from its mouth. The kitten sucked loudly at the nipple. She smiled up at Jeff. "I'd die if he did," she said.

"It would be hard. But at least we'd give him a chance. James Junior. doesn't seem to think he'll die though."

"Do you think it's a boy?" Amanda asked Jamie when he returned with the blanket and carefully wrapped the kitten up in it. It was sleeping now and looking very content.

"Yeah, he's a boy. It's easier to tell when they're tiny and they don't have much hair. Soooo.... what do you say? Will you help me out?"

Amanda looked at the tiny kitten wrapped up in the blanket sleeping happily in the palm of Jamie's large hand.

"How about I take him tomorrow after we finish here. I'll keep him during the day while you're at work. Then you can pick him up when you get off."

"I guess we could do it that way, but I sure could use a good night sleep tonight. I plan to get a lot accomplished tomorrow."

"Well ..."

"Amanda that's a lot of driving for James," Jeff said. "Remember we live half an hour north of town and he lives forty-five minutes south."

"Well ..." She took the bundle. "I guess I could keep him during the week. Then you could take him back on the weekend."

"It would just be until he's weaned. Then he can come back. I'll find him a home."

"I guess that would be okay. I hope he doesn't die."

"I don't think he will. Will you take him tonight?"

"Alright. But will you come to dinner one night this week? You can see how I'm doing and coach me if you need to."

"I don't think that's necessary."

"Please?"

"Well, I guess so. I'll get his kennel." Jamie ducked back into the hut.

Jeff opened the door and settled Amanda into the seat with the kitten. He went to the hut to take the carrier from Jamie.

"You know you'll never get that cat back."

"That's what I'm hoping."

*

"Alice," Jeff said when she picked up the phone that evening.

"Hey, Dad."

"The plan is in motion. Mom invited James Junior. to dinner one night this week. She didn't know she was helping us. You think you can get Ev there?"

"Sure. What night?"

"That's not decided yet. We're going out there to help work on a cat habitat tomorrow. We'll talk about it then. Is any night better for you?"

"Yeah, I'm usually off on Friday. I can ask my assistant manager to fill in for me if it has to be another night but it would be easier on Friday."

"Friday it is then."

*

"What do you mean you have a date?"

"I have a date on Friday night." Evelyn walked down the path to the far greenhouse with Alice behind her.

"You don't date. I don't ever remember you dating. Who are you going out with?"

"His name is Darren Drake. He's asked me out a number of times and I've said no. Now I guess I need to move on. Jamie is not going to change his mind. I have to accept that." She opened the door to the greenhouse and turned to look at Alice. "Are you sure you want to come in here? It smells like dirt and manure."

Alice pushed past her and sat on a stool. She crossed her arms and scowled.

"Oh, and for your information." Evelyn picked up a pair of garden gloves and slipped them on. "I have been dating since I was seventeen."

"You've been dating Jamie since you were seventeen."

"I dated other guys when I was at the university. Besides, Jamie doesn't want to see me anymore." She sat down on another stool across the potting table from Alice. "I don't think there will be anything romantic between Darren and me. But you can never have too many friends. Right now I don't have any friends."

"Sounds like you're feeling sorry for yourself."

"I guess I am."

"Couldn't you rearrange your date for another night? Mom and Dad wanted us to come out there that night. Dad said Mom is feeling better. She wants to show us something. He was kind of mysterious about it."

"Well, you can go without me. You can tell me what she wants to show us. Then I can go out on the weekend."

"Maybe we could go out there another night this week."

"Alice, you work nights remember. Friday is your only day off except Sunday. Maybe we could go Sunday."

"Okay, sure." She'd have to think of something. Jamie was coming on Friday. Either she'd have to get Evelyn there Friday or Jamie there Sunday. She stood to go. "I guess I'll see you later." She left the greenhouse relieved to get out into the fresh air. She didn't know how her Dad and sister stood it. They seemed to like that smell.

Alice walked around the outside of the building to catch a little fresher air. She reached the front steps to the café and started up.

"Evelyn," someone called from the parking lot. "She continued up the stairs, but the person called again. The sound of his voice was coming her way. Obviously, someone had mistaken her for Evelyn. She turned to see a handsome man, a very handsome man, hurrying toward her.

"I'm glad you're here. I was on my way out to get tickets for a movie Friday night. I wanted to make sure you like movies. Some people don't. I can get a general pass so we can choose which one we want to see. You didn't answer your phone. I hoped I could catch you here."

Alice's tongue seemed to be glued to the top of her mouth. She couldn't say anything. This guy was beautiful, really beautiful. His hair was black. His eyes were blue. His teeth seemed to glitter. She looked up at him. He must be six two with broad shoulders. And Evelyn doesn't think there will be anything romantic between them. Was she blind or stupid?

"I'm glad you caught me too," she said. Now this was just evil. "I was wondering if you could change the date to Sunday." Seriously evil. "I'm working in the evenings this week and I need to go to my parents' house on Friday. My Mom hasn't been well. I really need to go."

"Well I guess we could. Hey, are you okay? You look different somehow." He was studying her face. She could feel herself squirming.

"I'm just worried about my mom. I hope you don't mind the change. She turned to start up the stairs. He was making her nervous. "Maybe we could go to a matinee then to dinner. I actually love movies."

"Sure, okay." He smiled. "I'll call you with the details."

"Okay, but could you call me at a different number? I dropped my cell phone in the compost. I had to borrow one until I have time to get a new phone."

"Maybe that's why you didn't answer when I called."

"Must be. Do you have paper in your car?"

"I think so. I'll get it."

She gave him her number and hurried up the stairs to the café. She went straight to the office, closed the door behind her and leaned against it. "I just did a terrible thing."

"What was that?" David turned around in his chair.

"Ahh..." Alice jumped. "I didn't see you there."

"So, what is the terrible thing you did?"

"Not a big deal." She went to her desk chair. She hoped he couldn't see her heart pounding against her ribs. "I ordered the wrong napkins. I'll just order the right ones and send the wrong ones back when they come."

"Feeling a little dramatic today, Al? I really don't think I'd call that a terrible thing." David laughed and turned back to his work.

Alice fought the urge to put her head down on the desk. Instead she picked up her pencil and note pad.

*

"Ev." Alice stepped into the steamy greenhouse and tried not to gag on the smell.

"I'm worried about you, Al. You've entered a greenhouse twice in one day."

"I'm not happy about it but I needed to tell you something."

"Okay." Evelyn was obviously lost in the work she was doing.

"I ran into Darren. He thought I was you. I guess he doesn't know you have a twin."

"What did he say when you told him?"

"He asked if I'd tell you he had to cancel your date for Friday night. Something important came up."

"Really? That's too bad." She turned back to her work. "I hope he's alright. I'd call him but I've lost his telephone number. To tell you the truth, I was thinking of begging off and going to Mom and Dad's anyway."

Alice released a breath.

"I wonder why he didn't call me? Oh, he couldn't have gotten me. I left my phone on my desk."

Alice took another deep breath and released it. Hopefully she would be able to get to Evelyn's phone and erase any messages he might have left without getting caught.

"You know, Ev. I'm always scolding you for not keeping your phone with you. What if something happened to you. You need to be able to call someone."

"What's going to happen to me in the greenhouse. Besides, I don't like to be interrupted when I'm working."

"Well, I don't like it. I'll go get it for you."

"Don't you need to get to work. It's getting close to the rush."

"I can take time for this. It's important."

"Suit yourself."

*

Alice and Evelyn rode together to their parents' house on Friday. They chatted about their work. Alice laughed over Evelyn's story about her dirt fight with Darcy. Apparently, Darren and Evelyn hadn't talked during the week. Alice cringed a little at the thought. She knew eventually she would have to tell him she wasn't Evelyn. Not yet. She'd go out with him on Sunday but she'd tell him before they got started. That way he'd know. Maybe he'd go out with her anyway.

"What a tangled web we weave ..." She murmured as she looked out the window.

"What did you say?"

"Nothing, just talking to myself."

They pulled into the driveway. "Where did that wreck come from?" Evelyn asked as she pulled the shiny new Volkswagen up next to Jamie's car.

"I wonder."

They got out of the car and went into the kitchen door.

"Hey, girls." Amanda stood at the stove stirring a pot. She wiped her hands on her apron and hugged both girls. She smiled. Her smile still didn't quite reach her eyes. But it was the happiest she'd looked in a long time.

"You look like you're cheering up, Mom." Evelyn kissed her on the cheek.

"I am. Thanks to Albert."

"Who's Albert?"

"You'll have to go into the living room and see. He's in there with Dad and Jamie."

"Jamie's here!?" Evelyn stiffened. "Alice did you know about this?"

"I thought you said you'd talked to Evelyn and she was okay with it." Amanda scowled at Alice.

"This is a set up isn't it, Alice?"

"No of course not. I thought I'd told you. I mean with you having somewhere else to go and everything. I must have forgotten."

"Oh yeah, I really believe that." Evelyn picked up her purse from where she'd left it on the table.

"No, ma'am," Amanda said. "It would be rude to leave here. I didn't raise you to be rude. I suspect that Alice didn't tell Jamie you were coming either. Even though she said she would." She glared at Alice. Alice smiled sheepishly. "I suspect he wouldn't be here if she had."

Evelyn looked angrily at Alice. "I guess you didn't tell Darren who you were either. Did he even cancel the date?"

"Of course, I told him. Come on, Ev, give me a break."

"I don't know what you girls are talking about. I don't want to know. Just come into the living room and be polite." She started for the door then turned back. "Come on, girls, please. I really want you to meet Albert."

Evelyn relaxed her shoulders. It was obviously not her mother's fault, and whoever Albert was he seemed to be making her happy. She followed her into the room with Alice behind her.

Jamie sat in a wing backed chair holding a very small blanket. He looked up as they came in and gasped. He obviously tried not to look surprised but failed miserably. Amanda went to him, took the tiny bundle from his hands and brought it to the girls.

Any tension they had felt relaxed completely when they saw the tiny kitten.

"Oh, Mom." Evelyn took the kitten from her and looked down at it. "Look, Alice, his eyes are closed. His ears are just little nubs on the sides of his head."

"How old is he, Mom?" Alice moved the blanket aside to get a better look.

"Probably about a week by now. Jamie gave him to me on Saturday. He figured he was a few days old at that point."

"Jamie gave him to you?" Evelyn looked across the room at him. He stood self-consciously and shifted from foot to foot. He made an obvious effort not to make eye contact. Her heart thumped against her ribs. He's beautiful inside and out, she thought. I'll never stop loving him.

"Oh, he's fussing." Amanda took the kitten from Evelyn's hands. "I'll go warm his bottle. I can feed him while you fix yourselves a drink. Then we'll have dinner." She hurried back into the kitchen.

All four of them stood quietly for a second. Then Alice launched herself at Jamie, wrapped her arms around his neck and nearly knocked him over. He put his arms around her to steady himself and looked over her head at Evelyn. Their eyes met just for a second then he disengaged himself from Alice and stepped back.

"Jamie, that was perfect. Thank you." Alice said in hushed tones looking toward the kitchen.

"Yes thanks, Jamie," Evelyn said quietly.

"It wasn't much. I really did need someone to take that kitten. I just don't have time to do it right now."

"And she really needed to be needed right now." Evelyn turned to her dad. "She seems to be happy. Isn't that a relief, Dad?"

"Well yes. She's even said how happy she is to be needed again. I needed her. I guess that doesn't count." He was pouting.

Alice laughed. "Don't tell me you're jealous of a kitten, Dad."

"Of course not. That would be stupid."

Alice laughed. They all laughed. The tension between Evelyn and Jamie was building but there wasn't anything they could do about it.

"Where did you get a kitten that young?" She asked.

"I found him. I think his mom must have been feral. She probably had too many to support so she dumped the smallest one. I found him alone in the tall grass. No other kittens.

"And you brought him out here to Mom?"

"No. I gave him to her when they came out to see my place."

"They went out to see your place?" What was this? She looked at her dad. Was he in on this set up too? He looked innocent enough. But then he wasn't aware that she knew about it.

"That's right. Mom and I went out to get a look at the property he's going to develop into an animal rescue. He wants to do horses. I told him I'd share my experience with him. It's quite a place, Ev. I know Alice has seen it. Have you?"

"I don't know how I could have since I didn't know it existed." Okay, she was really pissed off now.

"I figured Marisa would have told you." Jamie kicked at the carpet with the toe of one shoe.

"No, Marisa didn't say anything about it either. I guess it doesn't matter though, does it? I think I'll have a drink, Dad."

"Okay, honey, what do you want?"

"How about a double martini."

"What?!" Everyone gasped and looked at her.

"I'm kidding, of course." She smiled, but she could feel the sarcastic expression on her face. "I'll just have a glass of wine. White."

"How about everyone else?" Jeff poured wine all around as Amanda came back into the room with the kitten and a miniature baby bottle.

"That is the cutest thing I've ever seen," Alice said. "Dad, have you taken pictures?"

"Actually, this is the most photographed kitten in the world. We have him sleeping. We have him drinking his bottle. We have him on the couch, on the bed, on the floor. We've got him just about everywhere in every position a kitten that young can be in."

"Have you got him in Mom's arms?" Evelyn asked.

"I don't like pictures taken of me."

"That's right. I forgot. Well, do you have him in Dad's arms?"

"Yes, his hands rather, Albert would fall right through his arms." Amanda laughed and glances were exchanged as she looked down at the kitten slurping loudly in her lap.

"How about taking a picture of him in my hands?" Alice asked.

"Sure." Jeff laughed. "Then we can take one of Evelyn, then James Junior., then all three of you."

Evelyn stiffened and the room went silent. Amanda looked up and frowned at Evelyn. She smiled and posed as Jeff snapped several pictures of the group.

"He's asleep." Amanda took the kitten from Alice and put him into his kennel. "Now we can have dinner. We're eating in the kitchen like old times."

Evelyn swallowed and followed everyone into the kitchen. Jamie pulled Alice's chair out then turned to Evelyn.

"Thanks, but I can seat myself."

"We went out on Sunday and helped James, Jr. build a cat habitat." Jeff said as they passed the food around. "You girls should come out and see it. It really is nice. We're going out on Sunday to work on the inside. We got the fencing up all around. You know you have to have it on the top, too. Cats can climb. This week we'll plant trees and plants for them to climb, small ones of course. We're also planning a cat walk. Why don't you girls come out and help."

"I'd love to, Dad. But I have plans already," Alice said. She looked down at her plate to hide the guilt she felt about her plans.

Evelyn looked at her guilty expression. This is another set up, she thought. "I don't think I'm invited. Apparently, Jamie doesn't want to include me in this little project."

"Evelyn!" Amanda said. "That was rude. Jamie is doing a very good thing here. You should be supportive."

"Oh yes, he's doing a good thing. Jamie always does good things. He's just so good!" She stood up and threw her napkin on the table. "Unless, of course, you're me!" She was shouting now. "Then you don't even rate a conversation. You don't rate any kind of explanations. You don't even rate being told something that apparently everyone else in the world knows. I should be supportive? He doesn't want my support!"

She turned around and picked up her purse and keys from the counter. "You do realize this is a set up don't you, James Junior."

Jamie winced at the use of his formal name. "What kind of a set up?" He looked around the room.

"That's right. What kind of a set up?" Amanda asked.

"Alice wants to get us back together." She looked at her sister.

"I don't know what you're talking about." Alice knew she looked innocent. She was a good actress. She looked at Jeff. It's a good thing he's not a poker player, she thought, I've never seen such a guilty look. Well, if he hasn't given himself away I won't get him in trouble.

"Oh yes you do. The thing is, Alice. Jamie doesn't want to get back together with me. I've accepted that. Why don't you? And you know what? I don't want to get back together with him either." She looked at Jamie and winced at the hurt expression on his face. If he didn't love her anymore why would he look hurt? She must have imagined it.

"I'm going now. Albert is beautiful, Mom. Thank you for showing him to me." She turned to leave.

"You can't leave. I rode with you." Alice said.

"Oh, I'm sure the good man over there will take you home." She stormed through the door, slamming it behind her.

The room was silent for a moment. They listened to Evelyn's car start and pull out of the driveway.

Jamie said, "I don't know what just happened here, but I think I'll leave, too."

"But Jamie, you haven't eaten," Amanda put her hand on his arm in a rare show of physical affection.

"Maybe you could fix me a to go box." He smiled at her. "I don't mean to be rude. I'm just tired and a little confused."

"Alright." She stood to get a plastic container and served him up some dinner. Alice stood up and picked up her purse.

"Mr. Landrum," Jamie said. "I wonder if you could run Alice home. I don't have a passenger seat."

Jeff laughed uncomfortably. "That's right. Sure. Sit down Alice. Eat your dinner. Then I'll take you home."

She sat back down and looked at her plate. Jamie gathered his box and left. They sat in silence again as they heard his car start, backfire then loudly move away.

"The next project is to replace that car," Jeff said.

"Alright." Amanda leaned against the counter and looked at Jeff and Alice. They both looked down at their plates. "What did the two of you do?"

Alice looked up and smiled. "I have no idea what she was talking about."

"You don't fool me with that innocent look, Alice. You're a good actress but you're not that good. And you, Jeff. An idiot couldn't miss the guilt on your face."

"Actually," Alice laughed. "I think Evelyn missed it and she's not an idiot."

"She didn't look at him. Now listen. This stops now. Let those two kids work this out themselves. I know they still love each other. But if they can't work this out they won't make it anyway. I mean it. Don't interfere again." Amanda left the room. They listened as she spoke quietly to the kitten. Then they heard her footsteps as she went upstairs.

"I think she's feeling much better." Alice smiled at her father's scowl.

"We messed up, Alice."

"We did."

Chapter 9

It was Sunday morning and Alice hadn't spoken to Evelyn since Friday. She hadn't wanted to talk to her at first because of her date with Darren and all, but by Sunday she was very uncomfortable. Okay, she hadn't sought Ev out but Ev hadn't tried to talk to her either. She must be really mad.

"I was only trying to help." Oh God, she was talking to herself now. "I'm going crazy. Well, of course I'm going crazy. I feel guilty. Not only did I try to manipulate my sister into the arms of one man. I stole her opportunity for another man."

She sat down on her couch and put her head in her hands. "I can't live with this," she said aloud. She stood and took her jacket off the hook. It was cool outside now. She left her apartment and headed across the complex to Evelyn's place. When she got there, she knocked on the door. Nothing happened.

"Oh, come on, Ev." She spoke aloud again and realized the only voice she'd heard that day was her own.

Heading back to her own apartment she dialed Evelyn's number on her cell phone. Still no answer. Was she blocking her calls or had something happened to her. She called her dad?

"Hey, Dad."

"Alice?"

"Yeah, have you talked to Evelyn since Friday?"

"Yes. She's here. She's at the barn with your mom. They're going riding. I'm kitten sitting."

"Wow, Mom really is feeling better isn't she?"

"She really is. I'm liking James Junior more and more these days."

"I thought you and Mom were going out to Jamie's this afternoon. Is Ev going too?"

"No. I'm following your mother's directions and not interfering anymore. Evelyn doesn't know the part I played in that disaster last week. I'm going to have to come clean with her. I'm eaten up with guilt."

"I know what you mean."

"You don't have to feel guilty. She knows you did it."

Not everything I did, she thought. "Well, she isn't speaking to me. That's why I called. I was worried something was wrong. But as long as she's okay, I guess I just have to wait until she forgives me. Got to go, Dad."

"Okay, honey. Talk to you later."

152 / Evelyn

Alice hung up the phone. She'd just call Darren and tell him the truth right now before he came to pick her up. He'd called to confirm their plans. His number was in her missed calls. She found it and held her finger over the number. She just couldn't tap it.

"I'll tell him as soon as he gets here. It'll be better in person. I've done a really bad thing. I need to make it right face to face." She put her phone back into her pocket and went into her apartment.

*

"Evelyn." Darren stood at Alice's door. "For some reason I thought you had one of the smaller apartments in this complex."

"There's a good reason for that." Alice waved him inside and closed the door.

"Listen," he said cutting off her confession. "I took a chance and bought tickets for the matinée at the symphony instead of the movie. I love the symphony. I have this feeling you and I are kindred spirits."

Whoa. She loved the symphony. "That's great! I love the symphony. I don't admit that to everyone."

"For some reason I thought so." He took the jacket she was holding and held it up for her to put on. "I hate the ballet. People always think if you like one you'll like the other. I don't. Do you?"

"No. I love the symphony but I don't like the ballet." It's funny, she thought, Ev loves the ballet. She doesn't like the symphony. Maybe this was just meant to be. No! She had to come clean. She opened her mouth to speak.

"One of the reasons I like the matinee is because it's short. I have a short attention span." Darren guided her to his car. "Then we'll go to dinner. I was thinking maybe we'd go to the café over the nursery. I haven't tried it. Is it good?"

Alice gulped. "It's great. But I go there all the time. Let's go somewhere else tonight."

"Okay, got any suggestions?"

"Well, there's a new steak place downtown. It's not far from Symphony Hall." All men like steak, she thought.

"I don't eat a lot of meat," he said. "I'm not a vegetarian or anything. I just don't eat a lot of meat."

How many times had she said that exact same thing? "I'm kind of the same way. There's this great Italian place close by there too."

*

"The symphony was fantastic," Alice said as they walked across the street to the restaurant. "I love it when the conductor talks about the performance before it."

"I do too." Darren put his hand on her waist to guide her protectively across the street. "I've seen her before. That's one of the reasons I wanted to see this. She's a visiting conductor. She's only here a couple of times a year."

I'll tell him the truth at dinner, Alice thought. She just couldn't do it when they were both enjoying the performance so much.

"Tell me about yourself, Evelyn," Darren said after they'd been seated in a corner booth ... at his request. "I've been attracted to you for a long time. Besides the fact that you're beautiful, I don't know anything about you."

Alice gulped. This was the time to come clean. "There's really not much to tell. I'm a little dull."

"I'm sure that's not true. Let's start with gardening. I know you love that. I like to play in the dirt too. I'm not very good at it though."

I'll deflect, she thought. "Why do you say that?"

"Well, I put in two shrubs this past spring. I'm pretty sure they're both dying."

"Hmmm," Wish I knew more about shrubs. "You should come to the nursery and get my sis ... my dad to help you with that."

"You wouldn't be willing to help me?"

"Sure. Sure, I would." That was a close one.

"I was thinking of putting in a pond. Maybe you could help me with that too."

"Sure. You have a house?"

"Yeah, I just bought one around the corner from here. Remember? I told you about it."

"Oh yes, I remember." Alice was thrilled when the waiter came to the table to take their order. "So, tell me about yourself, Darren. Are you from Atlanta?" She hoped he hadn't talked about this with Evelyn.

"No, I'm actually from Maine." He smiled. "I love it here. Atlantans have no idea how benevolent the climate is."

"I know it gets a lot colder there."

"You have no idea."

They rode back to her apartment in silence. Alice was so glad. She was more smitten with him now than she'd been before they went out. How would she tell him the truth? He wouldn't want anything to do with her when she did.

He pulled into a parking place in front of her apartment and got out of the car. Oh my God, he was coming around the car to open her door. She pulled it open and scrambled out. He took her hand and guided her toward her door.

"I had a great time, Evelyn." He took both of her hands and turned her toward him.

He was going to kiss her. She had to speak now.

"I hope you'll go out with me again," he said.

She nodded a little too energetically. He moved his lips toward hers. Now was the time to say something. She just couldn't. She closed her eyes and waited for the kiss.

"How far are you going to take this, Alice?" he whispered against her mouth.

She opened her eyes and looked directly into his. Her heart was thumping so hard against her ribs she thought one might break. "You've known all night?"

"I knew something wasn't right when I saw you last week. Of course, I didn't know Evelyn had a twin sister. But I noticed you were going up to the café so I called there and asked for Evelyn. I talked to your cousin, David I think he said his name was. He told me Alice owned the café and Evelyn worked in the nursery."

"I was planning to tell you as soon as you arrived tonight. But everything just seemed so right, the symphony and all. Did David tell you about that too?"

"No. I just had a hunch."

They were still standing close enough to kiss. Alice looked down and put her hands on his chest to push away. He held her close.

"I guess you don't want anything to do with me now," she said.

"I think you owe me a kiss." He tilted her head up and lowered his mouth to hers.

*

Alice sat at her desk the next morning. She could feel the stupid smile she'd been wearing all day. She hadn't had to be in until early afternoon. But she'd been too excited to sleep. The evening before had been so perfect.

She took a deep breath. How was she going to tell Ev about this? True. Ev hadn't been too keen on going out with Darren anyway. True. They really weren't compatible. But Alice had always been the one that wanted to be an individual. She hadn't wanted to be only a twin. She was the one who had insisted on wearing long hair so people could tell them apart.

Now she'd used their likeness to do a very underhanded thing. How would Ev take it?

Even with the guilt, Alice still had the goofy grin on her face when David came into the office.

"Want to tell me about what's making you look stupid?" He laughed. "It couldn't be that the heartless Alice has a heart after all?"

"Why would you say that?"

"I recognize the love-sick look. Is it the guy that called here asking for Evelyn the other day?"

"Yeah." She looked down at her desk and frowned.

"What happened?" David sat down at his desk and swiveled his chair around to face her. "You had that love-sick look on your face a minute ago. Now you're frowning. He couldn't have broken up with you in the past minute."

"No. David, I've done a terrible thing."

"Not a wrong order again. I already told you that's not a hanging offense."

"No. It wasn't a wrong order last week either." She looked up and directly into his eyes. "Darren asked Ev out for Friday night. He came by the nursery to ask her if she wanted to go to a movie. I was in the parking lot and ..."

"He mistook you for her."

"Right."

"You didn't correct him."

"I meant to. I really did. But ... well, Dad and I had plotted this little scheme to get Jamie and Ev back together. And one thing just led to another and somehow Ev's date with him on Friday night got turned into a date with him on Sunday."

"Only Evelyn didn't go on that date. You did."

"Right. Oh My God, David. It was fantastic. I really think I'm in love. I think he feels something pretty strong for me too."

"Only he thinks he feels this something strong for Evelyn."

"No, no. He knows I'm Alice now."

"Good. I'm glad your character is back to normal. Tell me you told him before you went out and had such an underhanded good time."

"I didn't tell him. You did."

"Really? He figured it out from our conversation?"

"Actually, he knew something was funny before he called you. That's why he called." Alice stood and went to the window. "Now I have to figure out a way to tell Ev."

"So, was Evelyn looking forward to this date?"

"No. She said she was thinking about canceling it. She likes him. But she'll never love anyone but Jamie. She was hoping for a friendship with Darren. That's all."

"So, what's the problem?"

"I'm ashamed of myself. Will she ever trust me again?"

"I'm sure she will if you come clean."

"Uh Oh." Alice's back stiffened. "Darren just pulled into the parking lot. I'll bet he came to talk to Ev."

"You'd better get moving if you want to do it before he does."

Alice was already out the door and down the steps. She went first to Evelyn's office. She wasn't there.

"Darcy." she hurried across the shop. "Where's Ev?"

"She's out in the propagation house. I just sent a very handsome young man out there. Evelyn's popular today."

Evelyn was in the back of the greenhouse when she heard the door open. She was hidden behind a shelf of seedlings. She couldn't see who it was.

"Is that you, Dad?" She called.

"No, Evelyn. It's Darren."

She suppressed a sigh and peeked out from behind the shelf. "Hey, Darren. I was meaning to call you." She'd actually completely forgotten about him. The broken date for the past Friday had been completely eclipsed by the trauma of that night. She stepped around the shelf and wound her way through the crowded greenhouse to the sink in the front. She took off her gloves and washed her hands. She was deliberately stalling. What would she say? She turned and smiled.

"I guess you've talked to Alice. Don't twins have some kind of telepathy or something? She probably didn't even have to tell you what happened." He sounded a little sheepish. He shuffled his feet uncomfortably.

"Well, she told me she saw you last week. That you had to cancel the plans for Friday." She looked at him cautiously. "You don't have to feel bad about it. I needed to go out to see my mom anyway. She hasn't been well."

He laughed. There was an awkward silence. "You haven't talked to her since then?"

"No." She had deliberately avoided Alice. She'd needed to let her temper cool.

"I didn't actually cancel that date. You did. Well actually, she did."

"I'm beginning to see what happened here. I'm sorry, Darren. Sometimes Alice can be a little bit interfering."

The door swung open. Alice stumbled in panting to catch her breath. She leaned back against the door and laughed.

"I guess you've told Evelyn about my little trick."

Evelyn smiled at her. "Darren was just telling me that you were actually the one who cancelled our date last week. Funny, Alice, you used to wear your hair long so that people could tell us apart. You said you wanted to be an individual, not just part of a set. Now you're pretending to be me." She laughed. "Oh well, no harm done."

"The thing is, Evelyn," Darren began.

"Ev." Alice put her hand on Darren's arm to stop him. "I did a little bit more pretending than that."

Evelyn narrowed her eyes. "What did you do?"

"I made a date with him for you on Sunday."

"You didn't tell me about it. How could I have gone?" She turned to Darren. "I'm sorry I stood you up, Darren." Her eyes flashed as she turned back to Alice.

"You didn't stand me up. You were there. Don't you remember?"

"Okay, stop it!" Alice stamped her foot. "He knew it was me he went out with. The thing is ... well ..."

"Alice stop stammering." Darren took her by the elbow and led her to the door. "I would like to talk to Evelyn alone. You can talk to her later."

Evelyn cringed inside. She didn't want to be alone with Darren. It had been a relief to have that date cancelled. She was going to have to tell him the truth. She didn't want to go out with him.

"I'm sorry about that," she said when he closed the door behind Alice. "Alice doesn't mean any harm. She's just always trying to run my life. Her heart is in the right place but sometimes her brain is out in left field."

"Listen, Evelyn. I'm not mad at Alice for that."

"Good. I'd better get back to work." She turned. She hoped the conversation would stop there.

"Evelyn, I've been attracted to you since the first time I saw you." She braced herself for his next invitation. "I've asked you out what, about fifteen times?"

"Something like that."

"Listen." He sat down on a stool next to where she stood and took her hand. She stiffened.

"Listen," he repeated. "I knew right away that Alice wasn't you. I didn't know you had a twin but something just wasn't right. I did a little bit of investigating and found out about your twin." He let go of her hand and stood up. He looked around the greenhouse then back at her. "I went on that date with her because I wanted to, not because I thought she was you."

"Whoa." Evelyn put her hand to her mouth and stepped back. She was trying to brush him off. He'd brushed her off instead. "I shouldn't feel so rejected. It wasn't going to work between us anyway."

"I'd pretty much accepted the fact that you didn't want to go out with me. I just thought maybe if I was persistent I could change your mind."

Evelyn laughed. "But now you've met Alice."

"Yeah, I'd like to pursue a relationship with her."

"Wow! Well. Okay, I guess." She sat down on the stool he had vacated and laughed. "Did she tell you who she was or did you catch her in the lie?"

"She let it go all the way to the end of the date. I don't know if she'd ever have told me if I hadn't called her on it."

"She'd have had to eventually."

A knock sounded on the door and Alice peeked around it. "So, I guess the whole story is out now?"

"Come in, Alice." Evelyn stood and crossed her arms. "Come in and explain to me why you pretended to be me and stole my man."

"I didn't mean to." Alice ran to Evelyn. "It just happened. I mean we just kind of hit it off, you know ... maybe it was ..." She looked at Darren and back at Evelyn. "I think I'll shut my mouth. I feel like I'm digging myself into a hole."

"Good plan." Darren stood and put his arm across Evelyn's shoulder. "Thanks, Evelyn." He kissed her cheek. "Friends?"

"Friends."

He turned back to Alice. "Evelyn says it's okay with her if I ask you out again."

"She does?" Alice looked up into his face. Evelyn could see their eyes meet in mutual attraction.

"Oh." Darren turned back to Evelyn. "I hope this hasn't hurt anything between you two. I really don't want to interfere with the trust between twins."

"Don't worry." Evelyn laughed and looked at Alice. "I never trusted her before. Why would I start now?"

*

"You owe me one." Evelyn stood in the doorway of Alice's office.

"You didn't like him anyway. Although I'll have to question your taste."

"I never said I didn't like him. I said it before, I think we can be friends. You can't have too many friends."

"Why would you want to be just friends with someone that looks like that?"

"Because I want more from someone that looks like Jamie."

Alice sighed. "I guess love blinds you. I thought you had decided to give up on Jamie."

"I have." Evelyn sat on the side of Alice's desk. "But I do think I owe him an apology. I said some mean things to him on Friday night. It wasn't his fault you hatched that stupid scheme."

"I didn't think it was so stupid at the time. I mean, the two of you in the same old setting. The one where your love first blossomed. How could it have gone so wrong?"

"This isn't a romance novel, Al. Anyway, I want to apologize to him."

"I have his number in my phone." Alice shuffled the papers on her desk looking for her phone.

"No," Evelyn said. "I have his number. But I'd like to tell him in person. Will you take me to his place? I can get away from work and dinner hour hasn't started here yet. I seem to remember Marisa telling me he doesn't have afternoon classes on Monday this semester."

"No way! Mom will kill me if I get any more involved in this. I'm surprised I got out of there on Friday without a bruised butt."

Evelyn laughed. "She did look mad. Her eyes were glowing red. It was good to see some life back in her. Did she chew Dad's butt out too?"

Alice looked sideways at Evelyn. "You knew Dad was in on it?"

"It would have been hard not to notice the guilt on his face. I'm surprised. I didn't think he liked Jamie much."

"I think he's always liked him okay. But lately they seem to be friends. And since Jamie brought Mom Albert he sees him in a whole new light."

"Come on, Al. Take me out there. Mom won't mind if I ask you to."

"Nope, I have too much respect for my flesh. I'll give you his address and some directions."

"I really don't want to go alone. I don't want him to think I'm plotting anything. I do have my pride, you know."

"Well, I'm not going to do it. Why don't you ask Marisa?"

"Maybe I will." Evelyn turned to leave. "Maybe Dad would take me."

"Nope, he's on restriction too, remember?" Alice watched Evelyn leave. When she heard the door to the shop close behind her she picked up the phone and punched in the number.

"Marisa," she said. "I hope you're available. The ball is in your court."

*

Marisa pulled her car into the gravel driveway of Jamie's place. "Boy, this really is rough."

"I can't believe you haven't been here before. I thought everyone knew about it but me." Evelyn rolled her window down and inhaled the fresh air. It was late October and it was cool outside, but she was warmly dressed and the air was clear and sweet.

"Actually, Jamie kept it a big secret. It was Alice that finally discovered it. After that I guess he figured he'd better come clean."

"Alice discovered it?"

"Uh oh, I guess I let the cat out of the bag. She hid in the back of his car. He brought her here without knowing it."

"Why did she do that? She's getting just a little bit out of control. I wish she'd stay out of my business."

"Don't be mad at her, Evelyn. She just loves you, that's all."

"Yeah yeah, I know. It's not like you to defend her though. The two of you haven't ever gotten along."

"We're getting along pretty well these days. I guess we've grown up."

"Maybe *you* have, but I don't think Alice will ever grow up." She decided not to talk about Alice's latest escapade. "Whoa, look at this place. It's beautiful."

"I'm not sure that's what I'd call it." Marisa pulled the car to a stop in front of the hut. The two of them got out.

"Well, that's what I'd call it. I guess Dad will get to landscape it when they get everything going."

"Don't look so disappointed, Evelyn. I'm sure he'll let you help.

"Look at the cat habitat over there." Evelyn jogged across the clearing to the caged yard and opened the gate to look in. "I can see Dad's fingerprints all over this place."

They stepped inside and went through the double gate.

"I guess that's there to keep the cats from escaping."

Evelyn looked around in awe. She couldn't speak. The cat walk was laced with hanging vines and air plants. There were shrubs and small trees.

"What do you think this plastic lining around the bottom of it is for?" Marisa asked.

"It's to keep the snakes out." They both jumped and whirled around as Jamie came into the habitat carrying two cages full of kittens. "What are you two doing here?"

"Hey, Bro." Marisa hugged him. "I'm here because I wanted to see the place. Evelyn is here because she wanted to talk to you about something. We figured we'd kill two birds with one stone and come in one car. I think I'll look around while you two talk. Meet me back at the car. Okay?"

"Yeah, I'll only be a few minutes."

Marisa left the habitat and walked toward the mobile homes. Alice watched her while Jamie put the cages down and stooped to release the kittens. The silence was uncomfortable until the playful kittens bounded out and started chasing bugs and rolling around with each other in play.

Evelyn found herself standing next to Jamie smiling at their antics. She looked up at him. He was smiling too. She wanted more than anything to put her arms around him. She moved her shoulders to shake the feeling.

"So, what did you want to talk to me about?"

She paused for a minute. She'd enjoyed being with him so much she didn't want to let it go.

"I wanted to apologize for the things I said to you the other night. It wasn't your fault Dad and Al are master manipulators."

"Oh, they're not such masters. It didn't turn out the way they planned it at all."

"No, it didn't." They laughed and looked back at the frolicking kittens.

"They're so happy," Evelyn said, a touch of sadness in her words. "They have no idea that they're homeless."

"They're not homeless. They'll stay here if nobody takes them. It's not the life I'd want for them but it's better than no life at all."

"Now see, there you go, being too good again."

"I'm not that good. In fact, I've made a huge mess out of this venture. I think David and your dad are going to pull me out of it. I hate that, but I'm not going to turn down their help."

They both turned at the sound of wheels on gravel and watched with open mouths as Marisa's car pulled out of the driveway. She waved out the window as she went.

"Well, I'll be damned," Evelyn said. "She's in on the plot too. Mom's going to kill Alice for this ... after I get finished with her."

"It's not like you to swear, Ev."

She looked back at him. "Oh yes it is. I swear all the time. It's you who never swears. You're just so good." She stormed to the gate.

"Damn Damn Damn." He laughed. "And a couple of Hells too."

She turned back and looked at him. Was he actually being friendly?

"Don't start another fight you'll have to apologize for, Ev. Apology accepted, by the way." He laughed and picked up the cages. "I'm just so good," he said as he went through the gate behind her.

"Listen, Ev, before you drive me back into town, how about a look around?"

"How am I going to drive you back into town. I don't have my car."

"You're going to drive mine. I don't have a passenger seat. There is only one seat belt. Your dad and I are getting along well these days. If you get hurt in my car because you didn't have on a seat belt, that'll be all over."

"So kind of you to think of him."

"I'm thinking of you too. So, how about it. A look around?"

"Okay."

"Where will you put the stable?" she asked after they had seen the kennel and cattery.

"Your dad says in the pasture land on the other side of the forest over there. You can't see it from here. I've made a path through the woods. It's rough. If you're game we could go see it."

"I'm game. Wow," she said a few minutes later when they came out of the woods to an open field. "How many acres do you have?"

"Twenty-five. There's another ten for sale at the back beyond the creek. If the loan comes through I'll look into buying it. I think there should be enough money. I guess it depends on how much they're asking."

"You could grow feed corn, maybe even some hay. It might not be enough, depending on how many horses you have, but it would certainly help."

"That's what your dad said. I don't know if I'll have the time though. I really hadn't planned to give up my job at the university. I doubt I can make a living here. Besides I like teaching tennis."

"You could still teach at the country club."

"I like teaching a competitive team, not spoiled rich kids."

"Like me."

He looked at her and brushed a stray hair off her brow. "Yeah, like you."

For just a second she thought he was going to kiss her. Wishful thinking. He stepped back.

"We'd better get back. It's getting dark early these days. I need to get the kittens in. Then I'll need to get you back to town before I feed and exercise the dogs."

"I could help you with the dogs."

He looked at her face. He seemed to consider it, then turned and headed back into the woods. "No," he said. "I'd better get you back to town."

*

"Earth to Evelyn. Earth to Evelyn."

She jumped and looked directly into Darcy's eyes. "I'm sorry. I drifted off for a minute."

"I noticed." Her tone of voice had changed since their little dirt battle. She was no longer so hostile. She could snap sometimes, but Evelyn remembered from way back that she was moody. "But if you don't help me get this bird food unloaded and stacked we won't have it done by the time your uncle gets here. Didn't we want to surprise him?"

"Yes, we did. He wanted to help with arranging the shelves and the displays, but I think he'll be happy to see that we've filled the shelves."

"Then snap to. We've got a loading dock full of seeds."

Evelyn poured herself into her work.

"Want to talk about it?" Darcy asked after a few more loads of seed.

"I'm not sure there's anything to talk about."

"It's that boy, isn't it? Sometimes I'd like to wring his neck."

Evelyn laughed. "I didn't know you felt so strongly about it. I didn't even know you knew about it."

"Of course, I know. I lived with your daddy's black moods until he came to terms with it when you were kids. And the boy always promising not to take advantage of your innocence. There was no doubt in my mind who was taking advantage of who."

Evelyn laughed again, this time sitting down on a pile of seed bags. "Now why would you think I'd be the pursuer?"

"I've been young and in love. Hell, I've been old and in love. Men might be attracted but if you're really interested you have to push."

"Darcy, how many times were you married?"

"Only two. They lasted a pretty good little while too. Both of them."

"What happened?"

"I love my work." She looked around the huge room full of plants, displays of pots, and now bird feeders and houses. "I love this place. I guess neither one of my husbands loved me enough to share me with it. I guess I didn't love them enough to give it up."

"Could they have supported you if you had given it up?"

"Oh yes, they both had money. What happened is they both wanted a wife that would stay at home and make the place nice, cook their meals, look good at parties." She laughed. "... buy their underwear."

Evelyn laughed. "I really can't see you in that role."

"I can't see it either. I loved them both though. Sometimes I think maybe that was fate. I wouldn't have had the chance to love Andy, the second husband, if it had worked with George, the first."

Evelyn sighed.

"I get the feeling that James Junior is going to be your one and only."

"I do too."

"I take it part of the problem is that James Junior can't support you. He's hung up on that."

"That's what Marisa says. I guess he talks to her. You know, he doesn't have to support me. I don't plan to give up my career any more than you did."

"Does he have a problem with that?"

"I don't think so. He's always been very supportive." She frowned. "I mean before I went away to school. He stopped seeing me after that. I don't know what to do. I had decided to leave it alone. If he doesn't want me then I don't want him."

"That's not an option."

"No, it isn't." Evelyn picked up a bag of bird seed and tossed it onto the shelf just a little bit too enthusiastically. The shelf went over backwards. The shelf behind it went over backwards. The shelf behind that went. It was a clear game of dominos ending with the loud clanging of the bird shaped wind chimes at the end of the room.

"Hey, guys," Brian said as he came into the room. He stopped short. "What happened?"

Darcy turned to look at him. "Evelyn happened."

*

"Now see this?" Bradley called to Evelyn from where he was perched on the side of the cliff in the Martin's back yard. He pulled a tennis ball out of the small pack he wore around his waist and put it on the back of the ledge. It promptly rolled off. "There is no way you can plant anything here. It'll wash away in the rain."

"Bradley, come down from there." She held her breath.

"I believe I told you not to call me Bradley." He stood and she sucked in a breath, praying that he wouldn't fall.

"Brad, please come down from there. You might fall."

"I won't fall. Look, I'll show you the ledge the vine will work better on."

Evelyn squeezed her eyes closed then opened one a crack to watch as he scaled the wall to a point about 6 feet higher than the first ledge. "You told your parents you weren't stupid enough to climb that wall."

"I said I wasn't stupid enough to climb the cliff and go into the traffic. I have to climb the cliff."

"Why do you have to climb it?"

"I just do. Don't worry. I usually bring my rock climbing equipment."

"Scary, isn't it?" Ruth approached from behind and handed her a bottle of water.

"I don't know why you haven't died of a heart attack."

"It did take some getting used to. But he really is quite capable. I watch closely though. Accidents can happen to anyone."

"See this ledge, Ev," Bradley called. He put another tennis ball on the tip of the rock and it rolled back out of sight. "See it really has sort of a natural hole up here to plant in. The crevice in the rock collects dirt. I think the roots of the vine will be able to spread enough to support the plant. It could cover most of the cliff."

"I believe you. The landscaping team can get up there and that's where we'll plant the vine. Now would you please come down?!"

"Come on down, Bradley," Ruth called. "I need to run a few errands. You need to come with me."

"Aww, Mom," he pouted. "I hate going all those places with you."

"Come down, Bradley."

"What places are you going that he hates so much?"

"The grocery store, the dry cleaner, etc. He hates it." They watched as Bradley gracefully scaled the cliff to the ground.

"Can't I stay here with Evelyn?" He turned to look up at her. "You'll be here for a while, won't you?"

"Not more than a few minutes. I have to get back to the nursery. I've got some work to do in the greenhouse."

"I could go with you. I'd much prefer that."

Evelyn laughed. The kid was just too smart for a four-year-old. Prefer, she was sure she hadn't used that word when she was four.

"No," Ruth said. "Now run inside and wash your hands and clean the dirt smudge off your face before we go."

He put his hands in his pockets and walked away with his head down and his shoulder's bent. He looked like a grumpy old man.

"You know..." Evelyn looked back at the sketch pad she was holding. "He could come with me if he really wants to. Although, I understand if you don't like him riding in the car with other people.

"He goes to a playgroup three times a week in a carpool. I can't give a driving test to everyone he gets in the car with, but Evelyn, you don't need to babysit my kid."

Evelyn laughed. "I can't relate the term babysit to Brad in any way. He did help me with these plans. Let me take him. He might enjoy it."

"Okay, if you're sure. I'll get things done a lot faster that way. I'll pick him up at the nursery in about an hour and a half, maybe two. Is that too long?"

"No, that'll be great. I need about another half hour here. Then we'll head over there. Oh but, Ruth. Will you tell him no rock climbing while you're gone?"

Ruth laughed. "I'll tell him. I wouldn't want you to die of a heart attack."

A few minutes later Bradley came running out of the house. "Thanks, Ev. Can we go now? I've never been in a greenhouse before."

"Just a few more things I want to look at here. Your mom told you not to climb, right?"

"She really didn't have to tell me, Ev." She smiled at his use of her nickname. "I'm not stupid enough to kill the goose that laid the golden egg. I know if I don't behave properly I won't get to go with you again."

Evelyn turned to him and lowered her sunglasses. "Brad, where do you get your vocabulary?"

"The goose and the egg come from a fairy tale. Every kid knows that. The rest, well, I read a lot."

"You read a lot," she murmured and turned back to the rock wall. "You know what, Brad, the ledge we had originally planned for that trumpet vine might be good for a fountain. It would look very natural, not tacky to please your mom. We could put a small basin in at the base of the hill. The splashing sound would make your dad happy. I'm just not sure how we would pipe it."

She turned to look at him. He stood with his back to her. His hands were clamped tightly over his ears.

"You're going to have to come to terms with it, Brad. Your parents are in charge. There will be a fountain."

"Stop talking about it. Now I have to go back in and pee." He reached into his pocket, pulled out a key and ran to the back door.

*

When Evelyn and Bradley walked into the nursery, Marisa, Helen, and Alice had their heads bent together over a display of tropicals.

"Okay, what are the three of you planning?" Evelyn said. Alice jumped back. Her poker face was getting rusty.

Marisa looked up. "I came here to apologize. That was a pretty dirty trick I pulled on you the other day. I'm sorry."

Evelyn looked at Helen. "I don't know what any of you are talking about, Helen said."

She looked so sincere that Evelyn laughed and turned to Marisa. "I guess I can forgive you since I'm pretty sure I know who put you up to it." She glared at Alice.

"What are you talking about?" Alice held her hands out palms up.

"You know, Al. Your poker face is slipping. You have the same guilty look on your face Dad had last week."

"Well, I'm innocent this time. Dad and I are staying out of your love life. You know how it feels when Mom looks at you with her eyes glowing red."

"Who's your friend?" Helen asked.

Evelyn looked around. Bradley was across the room standing against the wall. His eyes were squeezed shut and his hands were over his ears. It took her a minute to realize they were standing next to the fountain display.

"That's Brad. I'm showing him around the nursery today." She lowered her voice. "Fountains make him feel like peeing. He's in distress right now because his parents are putting in a fountain. He's afraid he'll wet his bed."

"Poor kid." Helen started in his direction.

"Brad," Evelyn said. She followed Helen hoping she wouldn't say anything about his problem. "This is Mrs. Morris. She's a good friend of mine."

"It's nice to meet you, Mrs. Morris." He held his hand out to her. "Any friend of Ev's is a friend of mine."

Helen glanced at Evelyn and smiled as she shook his hand. "Well, I'm glad to hear that. Do you like to garden?"

"My dad is really the gardener. I've helped Ev with some plans for landscaping our back yard. It presents some rather unusual challenges."

"Really? Tell me about them."

"I'll let Ev do that some other time. She's about to show me the greenhouse. It will be a new experience for me. I've never seen one before."

"Wow," Helen said. Evelyn smiled and guided Bradley in the direction of the greenhouses.

"Catch you later, Helen."

Jeff was working at the potting bench in the back of the greenhouse. He turned as they came in. "Well hello, Brad." He stood and approached them with his hand stretched out. "Have you come to check out the fountains?"

Bradley squeezed his eyes shut and put his hands over his ears. Jeff exchanged a look with Evelyn then stooped to eye level with the child.

"Is it that bad?"

"You just don't know." Bradley opened his eyes and lowered his hands. "I can't even stand to look at the watering can when Dad waters the plants in the house." He leaned forward and spoke quietly. "You know what the spout on the can looks like."

Evelyn gasped then covered her mouth quickly. Jeff looked up.

"You know," Jeff stood and guided Bradley over to the potting bench. "When Evelyn's cousin David was a boy, he used to stay with me in an apartment we had upstairs. His bedroom was right next to the fountain display. I never understood why he always looked so tired the next day."

"He was afraid to go to sleep because he might wet the bed."

"I understand that."

Jeff picked him up and put him on the bench. "Look at that plant." He pointed to an air plant that hung from the ceiling. "That plant doesn't need to have its roots in water. It takes all its nourishment from the air."

"Wow, really?" Bradley reached up and felt the plant. "It's thick and kind of spiky."

"We moved David to the room across the hall. He did fine after that."

"Dad," Evelyn said. "I'm not sure David would appreciate you telling him about this."

"Why not? It's nothing to be ashamed of."

"Did he ever get over it?"

"Yeah, we used to like to camp. We always camped next to a stream."

"Ahhhh ..." Bradley squeezed his eyes shut and clamped his hands over his ears.

"It worked best to camp next to the stream. Then you could wash your mess kit when you finished dinner without having to tramp through the woods in the dark."

Bradley opened one eye. "I guess that makes sense."

"Look over here, Brad." Jeff lifted him off the table and crossed the room with Bradley in tow. "These are what you call succulents. They need very little water at all. They store it in their leaves and stems, sometimes in their roots. In the desert people use them as sources of water."

"They have thorns. How do you get the water without getting stuck?"

"You handle them very carefully. Come on, Brad. I'll take you out to the yard. You can water the winter crops."

"Ahhhh ..." Bradley squeezed his eyes shut and covered his ears. Jeff smiled at Evelyn and led the child out the door.

She worked for about an hour, worrying all the time that she should check on Bradley. Silly, she thought. Her dad was capable of taking care of the boy. Finally, tired of resisting the urge, she went to look for them.

They were in the quarry. That was what they called the yard where they kept stones and garden rocks. Darcy was standing with them, a scowl on her face.

"Jeff," Darcy said. "Don't tell me you're bringing kids in here again. You know it really isn't safe to have a boy this young climbing on the rocks. What if he gets hurt?"

"I won't get hurt?" Bradley huffed. "I'm gifted athletically as well as intellectually."

Darcy looked down at him for a minute before she spoke. "That may well be, but if one of those paving stones falls on you you'll be smashed."

"Darcy, I'm not going to let a paving stone fall on him. Now let us finish what we were doing." Jeff stood looking at Darcy with his arms crossed.

"What *are* you doing, Dad?"

"I'm helping Brad choose stones for the base of the fountain. He told me about your suggestion of the spot for it. It sounds perfect to me."

"The question is..." Bradley looked up at Evelyn. "Should the stones at the base be a more natural look to blend with the rock face, or should there be a contrast between past and contemporary, wild and civilized, natural and manmade, you know?"

"This is a fountain we're talking about, Brad. You know that, right?"

"Ahhhh ..." He squeezed his eyes shut and covered his ears then recovered quickly. He tugged a little at the front of his pants and looked up at Jeff. "I'm getting there."

*

Evelyn looked around the shabby office waiting room. The business was a Primary Care Clinic. They wanted her to jazz it up. That was their wording. The upholstery on the chairs was not torn or shabby in any way. It was just ugly. It did look somewhat worn. It was certainly not new. The color on the walls was drab. She called colors like that *institutional colors*. Why did all institutions feel like they needed drab walls? They weren't calming. They were depressing.

Putting some plants in some strategic places would certainly liven it up. In order to really *'jazz it up'* she'd have to bring in a rain forest. She thought of Ruth. She really hadn't done much about the interior design business she was thinking about. Maybe she was too busy with Bradley. He was a handful. Maybe, though, she would be interested in starting small with a place like this.

"Any chance you have room in the budget for some redecorating?" She asked the office manager who stood next to her.

"We were hoping some plants would do the job."

"They would certainly help. You could use a coat of paint and some reupholstering done at least."

"We can stretch it some I think. I'd have to get it approved. When we first decided to jazz the place up we had an estimate for redecorating. I'd have to look for a different decorating firm. No way we could afford that."

"I might know someone. She's just starting out. She might be willing to give you a break in the price."

"Okay, bring her in. We'll review it and see what we can afford. I wouldn't want to interfere with your budget, though.

We really believe that plants would make a difference in our patient's attitudes."

"No, don't interfere with my budget." Evelyn laughed. "I'll ask her if she's interested and get back to you."

*

Evelyn arrived at the Martin's house about an hour later. The crew had started work the week before. It was getting late in the fall to put in most plants, but the small front yard could be finished. They could seed it with winter grass. That would do well in the fall and winter. Adam had opted to go with Fescue. He knew that it tended to burn in the summer, but enjoyed the green lush grass in the winter. They'd try it for a year or two. If the summer burn bothered them, they'd change to a summer grass even though it would go dormant in winter. The shrubs and trees could be put in now, too. The back yard would have to wait until spring. They could do some preparation now, though.

She had a few words with the foreman of the crew. It looked like he had everything under control. The garage door was closed, but she could see through the window that Ruth's car was there. She rang the doorbell and waited for Ruth to open the door. Bradley opened it instead.

"I'm glad you're here," he said as he ushered her into the house. "I'm working on my design for the fou ... Well, you know what."

"Still can't say the word, huh?"

"I said it once earlier. I don't want to push my luck."

Evelyn followed him into the office that was off the kitchen. There was a computer on with a drawing program on the screen. There were some elaborate lines and circles on it. Evelyn couldn't make them out until Bradley started to explain them to her. Then they became quite clear.

"That looks great. You know, Brad, I don't use a computer. I draw my plans. Maybe you could help me learn the program." She laughed. She was asking a four-year-old to teach her.

"It might help, but some people are more artistic than me. Pencil and paper works better for them."

"I thought you were gifted."

"In athletics and intellect, not art. You can't have everything, Ev." He sat back. "So, what do you think?"

"You know, Brad. I think I'm one of those people. I'd like to learn the program but I just don't think I can really get a good idea of it unless I draw it out."

"That's what I figured. I'll print them out for you. Mom's in the laundry room on the other side of the kitchen. I'm sure you came to talk to her, not me."

"I like talking to both of you." She squeezed his shoulder and left the room.

"Hey, Ruth."

"Aaaa ..." She jumped and put a hand on her chest. "You startled me."

"I'm sorry. You must have been deep in thought. I didn't tip toe."

"I was. So, what can I do for you." She folded her last towel and went into the kitchen. "Let me get you some coffee."

"No thanks. I've had about four cups. I'm already buzzing. How about a glass of ice water?"

"Alright. You must taste these tea cakes I made. It's the first time I've made them. It won't be the last. They're wonderful."

"Ruth, I have this office job. You know I've been trying to rebuild our corporate business. Dad's partner had a good business going. When she retired a few years ago, Dad let it go. It's not his thing."

"How's it going?"

"It's a little slow. I do have this job going right now. They've approved my design and budget, but the place really needs a decorating job."

"I think I know where you're going. I appreciate it, but I really have my hands full with Bradley. I don't think I can find the time. You know he's home schooled so he's here most of the time. He has a couple of social events with the home school association each week, but that time fills up really fast."

"I think you should do it, Mom." Bradley stood in the doorway to the office. "You need a little distraction. So, do I. We're beginning to annoy each other."

Evelyn looked at Ruth. "Where does he get his vocabulary?"

"He watches TV with a dictionary in his lap."

"I don't need it for much," he said. "I can get most of the meanings from context."

"I'm sure you can." Evelyn looked at Ruth again. "How about it? Bradley thinks you should. He can live without you for a few hours a week. It'll be an easy job. They don't have a big budget."

"I can't exactly take Bradley with me."

"You can find a ba ... You can find a sitter. There are agencies for that."

Ruth sat looking at Bradley for a minute. "I suppose I could pay for it with the money I earn from the job."

"That's right. Then if you decide to do more, you'll make more than a sitter costs."

"I have a better idea," Bradley said. "I could go to the nursery and stay with you. I promise I wouldn't get in the way."

"Oh, Bradley." Evelyn felt bad to say no. "I love it when you come to the nursery. You never get in the way. But I'm not always there. I have appointments. Sometimes I have paperwork to do. I'm afraid we couldn't make it a regular thing."

He stuck out his bottom lip. Tears filled his eyes. He really is just a child, she thought.

"Honey, it wouldn't be too many hours with a sitter," Ruth said. "And you could use the time to get some of your projects done." She turned to Evelyn. "He's always doing something. Right now he's designing a computer game."

"Wow, really? I'd like to see it. I'm not very good at those games, but I've never met a designer before."

"You can't see it. I hate you." He turned and fled the room. They could hear him crying as he pounded up the steps.

Evelyn said, "Let me ask some of the other people at the shop. Maybe they would be willing to watch him when I'm not there."

"No. He has to learn that just because he has some gifts doesn't mean he can always have his way. He has to have limits just like any other child."

"It's really hard, isn't it?"

"Yeah. I love that kid so much. I'd like to give him everything he wants but I can't. I guess all parents deal with that."

They heard a sniffle and turned to looked at the doorway. Bradley stood there mopping his eyes with his shirt. "How about we compromise," he said. "When you're going to be in the shop and Mom needs to be gone, I could come. When you have an appointment, we could get a sitter. You usually know your schedule, don't you?"

"Usually. Sometimes I have to leave unexpectedly. We could designate a couple of times a week when I could commit to being there." She looked at Ruth who was giving her a punishing look. "Compromise is important to learn, too."

"I suppose so. We can try it but, Bradley." She looked directly into his eyes. "If it doesn't work for any of us, you will accept it, understand?"

"Yes, ma'am." He turned and ran back up the stairs.

"Ev, your kids are going to be so spoiled."

*

"Why is the kid here again?" Darcy looked sour.

"He's just hanging out. He likes it here. Maybe he'll grow up and go into the business." Evelyn thought it would be better not to go into the details of the arrangement.

"Well, keep him out of the way."

"I never get in the way, Darce." Bradley was helping to arrange some wind chimes.

"My name is Darcy."

"I know." He didn't look at her.

Brian approached from the back of the section. "He never does get in the way, Darcy. In fact, he's very helpful. And I'm not just saying that to please a child. He's helping me with a design for a humming bird garden. I'm thinking of putting one in out back."

"What do we need with a humming bird garden?" Darcy's mood was deteriorating.

"Well we don't need one. I just think it would be nice for the customers to see what they can do with the plants and the wild bird supplies we sell. We'll use hummingbird feeders."

"That reminds me Brian," Bradley said. "I'd like to show you some changes I've made to the plans. Judging from the angle of the sunlight some of the plants need to be put in different places. I'm glad we haven't started planting yet. Of course, we won't start until spring."

"You've learned a lot about the plants, haven't you?" Brian smiled down at him. "I never could keep them straight. I guess that's why Jeff went into the business and I didn't."

"I guess. Maybe when you get a chance you could come into my office. I'll show you what I've done."

"Brad," Evelyn laughed. "You do know that's my office."

"Yeah, but I like to pretend."

Darcy shook her head in disgust and walked away.

Bradley watched her leave. "I'll go pester her in a little while."

"Don't push your luck. Remember what your mom said."

Someone came down the steps from the café. They all turned expecting to see Alice. It was Jamie. He was dressed in sweatpants and a t-shirt. There was a hoodie draped over his arm. He approached the group and smiled at Evelyn.

"Hello, Jamie," Evelyn said. "I'd like you to meet Bradley. He's a good friend of mine."

"I prefer to be called Brad." He glared at her and extended his hand to Jamie.

Jamie smiled and shook his hand. "It's nice to meet you, Brad. How are you, Ev?" He shuffled his feet and looked down.

"I'm fine. What are you doing here?"

"I had to sign some papers for the loan. I came between lessons so I need to go now."

"What kind of lessons?" Brad asked.

"Tennis."

"Really. I've always wanted to learn how to play tennis."

Jamie looked down at him. "Always can't have been a long time."

"I get it. Yes, I am only four. I'm gifted."

"I can tell."

"Would you give me lessons? I'm sure my mom will say it's okay."

"Maybe in a few years. I think you're a little young."

"You might be surprised, Jamie." Evelyn laughed. "Brad is gifted athletically as well as intellectually."

"I don't think he can hold a racket. I doubt he could find one his size."

"I think I could design one. I don't know about building it. Jeff probably could."

"Work on it. We'll talk when it's done. Well, better go. See you Ev. Nice to see you, Brian." He left and Evelyn turned back to her work.

"He came down those back steps hoping to see you," Brian said.

"I don't think so. He just didn't want the lunch crowd to see him in his tennis clothes."

*

"So, Darce." Bradley sat on the chair next to her desk.

"My name is Darcy."

"Is that Jamie guy Evelyn's boyfriend?"

"Used to be." Darcy was deep into a computer spread sheet.

"Seemed to me like he liked her pretty much."

"When did you meet him?"

"Earlier. He came down from the café and stopped to say hello. He shuffled his feet like he was nervous. His face turned red."

"Jamie's shy and fair skinned. His face turns red a lot."

"So why isn't he her boyfriend anymore?"

"Because he's an idiot." Darcy looked up at Bradley like she had just realized he was there. "Beat it, kid. I'm working and I'm not a gossip. So, if you want info you'll have to go somewhere else."

"Okay." He hopped down from the chair. "I have some work to do on Ev's computer anyway. Thanks for the info, Darce."

"My name is Darcy."

Half an hour later Evelyn looked into her office. "I'm glad you're still in here. I shouldn't have gone so long without checking on you."

"I told you I had work to do."

"Are you doing homework?"

"No, that was done a long time ago. And you know, Ev. I'm home schooled. So, all of my work is homework."

"That's true. Let me see what you're doing then." She walked around the desk so she could see the computer screen. "Wow, Bradley, you never cease to amaze me." There was a graph of a tennis racket. Beside it a graph of another one on a larger scale.

"My biggest problem is to make the head of the racket as big as the original without making it too top heavy to hold with a smaller handle."

"I'm sure you'll manage. You really want to take lessons don't you."

"Yeah, if I can talk Jamie into teaching me. You know it's hard to get grownups to take you seriously when you're four years old."

"I guess. I think he'll teach you. But if he won't we'll find someone else. I'm sure your parents would be okay with it."

"We'll start with Jamie. Hopefully he'll say yes."

"Hopefully. Listen, Brad. They're delivering the blocks for the fountain to your house today."

"Ahhh ..." He covered his ears with his hands and closed his eyes.

"I thought you were getting over that. You're the one that designed it."

"I'm getting better but I really have to go."

"Well, go then. You know where it is."

"I didn't want to stop my work." He called over his shoulder as he ran out of the room.

Evelyn laughed and looked again at the computer screen.

"Hey, honey." Jeff put a hand on her shoulder. "What are you looking at with that look of wonder on your face?"

"Brad is designing a tennis racket for someone his size. Look at this, Dad. That kid is amazing."

He looked at the screen. "He is. He's a nice boy, too. I think he's getting over his problem with the fountain."

"Actually, he just ran out of here to the bathroom because I mentioned the blocks were being delivered today. He said he already had to go."

"Well, I can understand that. We have to keep reminding ourselves that he's only four years old."

"I know you're talking about me." Brad stood in the doorway. "I'm the only four-year-old around here."

"Yes, we were talking about you." Evelyn turned to face him. "I was going to tell you that I'm going over to have a look at the delivery, make sure everything is right. The crew will get started on it tomorrow. I've already called your mom and told her I'll bring you home. I thought you might want to have a look at it, too."

"Are they going to start the piping tomorrow, too?"

"Yes, they have to do that first."

"I hope I'm ready for this." Bradley shook his head and looked very concerned. "Jeff," He turned and looked up. Evelyn was always amused when Brad called adults by their first name. It was funny with the contrast in sizes. Jeff at 6 feet 3 and Brad at 3 feet 6. "Do you think you could build this tennis racket? I can give you all the measurements."

"I'm not gifted, remember?" Jeff laughed. "You should ask Jamie. I doubt he could build it, but he might know where you could have one custom made. It might cost a lot, though."

"Hmmm. Ev, could you call him for me?"

Evelyn looked at him suspiciously. "Don't tell me you're plotting, too?"

"What do you mean?"

Okay, she thought, no one could fake that innocent face. It was silly to think he was involved. "I'll tell you what. I'll give you his number and you can call him. I have it in my phone. I just have to remember where I left my phone."

"Honey..." Jeff kissed her temple. "You're hopeless."

*

"I guess they liked your price for the waiting room. Are you getting paid enough to make any profit?" Evelyn and Ruth were sitting on the patio that had just been finished the day before.

Ruth poured some piping hot tea. "It's getting cold. Are you sure you're warm enough out here? We can go into the kitchen. I can see Bradley from the breakfast nook. That's one reason we put in all those windows."

"I'm fine, except watching him scale that wall is making me very nervous."

"I'm pretty used to it, but it still makes me nervous." She sipped the steaming liquid. "They seemed to be okay with the price. You know, puckered brows and deep sighs. I couldn't have taken anything off price-wise, though. If I had I'd be paying for it myself."

"Maybe you shouldn't do it. I didn't mean to get you into a losing situation."

"No no, I'm excited about it. You have to start somewhere. I have some really good ideas. I need to get together with you and look at your plans for the plants. We'll need to coordinate that."

"Yeah, and that brings up another subject. I wonder if we couldn't work together on that. Kind of a networking thing. I recommend you when I have a chance. You recommend me when you have a chance. Then we could work together. We'd be the best decorating business in town."

"You haven't seen my work yet."

"I've seen your house. You like my landscaping plan. Obviously you have good taste." They laughed.

"That sounds like a great idea. I have to admit, I've thought about it myself. But for now, it's just a thought. I have to see how this goes. It might be too much with trying to keep up with Bradley. What about you? Do you have time for something like that?"

"Sure, I'm planning to grow the corporate business anyway. When it starts making money I plan to hire people to help. I'd still do all the planning. I could train people to maintain it. I hope to have a team that can install everything. Maybe even a sales person."

"You're very ambitious. We'll think about it. Let's see how this goes."

*

Evelyn headed toward her apartment. She smiled. Bradley had insisted on going to the bathroom before he went outside to check out the delivery. It was good because he didn't have any problem. He even discussed the project with the foreman of the crew. She laughed. It was always so funny to see the look on the face of someone who talked to Brad for the first time.

She parked the car and got out. She pulled her jacket around her face to protect it from the cool breeze. Winter was coming on a little early this year. In Georgia, it usually wasn't this cold in the end of October. She looked at the sky. There were dark clouds forming in the west. There must be a storm moving in. She turned at the sound of her name and spotted Darren hurrying toward her.

"Hey, Darren. I'm pretty sure Alice is working tonight."

"She is." He smiled as he reached her. "That's the problem with dating a restaurateur. You don't get to do a lot of evening dating. And of course, I'm busy during the day, so we have to squeeze time in where we can."

"Well, come in and have something with me. I'm not Alice, but I'm still pretty good company."

Darren laughed and opened the door for her after she unlocked it. "I'll appreciate the company. In fact, I was hoping you'd come over to the café with me. We could sit at the bar and have dinner. Maybe we could get a few minutes of Alice's time."

"It's a nice offer, Darren, but I'm tired. I think I've seen enough of the place for one day."

"I understand. I would like to come in for a minute, though. I'd like to talk to you about something."

"It sounds serious. What would you like? I was going to make some coffee. I have a wonderful cinnamon infused one, caffeine free. It's too late in the day for caffeine."

"That would be great. It'll warm me up. It's kind of a wicked night out there. I think we're going to have rain."

Evelyn went to the kitchen behind the breakfast bar. "I think those look like snow clouds. Of course, I don't know what a snow cloud looks like."

"It's too warm out there to snow. I know that wind makes it seem cold. It isn't really."

"Sounds like you have experience. Are you from the north? You don't sound southern."

"I'm from Maine. Maine accents are very strong. I've lost some of mine."

"What are you doing here?"

"I'm working at Georgia Tech. I'm teaching while I get my Masters. I went to Georgia Tech for my engineering degree, electrical. I liked it so much I stayed after I graduated."

"That's nice." She put the coffee on the bar and two mugs. "Do you take cream and sugar?"

"Black is fine."

"So, what did you want to talk to me about?" Sugar came out of the bedroom, stretched and yawned, exposing a mouthful of shiny white teeth.

"Hey, pussy cat." Darren put his hand down to let the cat sniff. Sugar hissed and jumped up onto the bar. "Nice cat." He smiled at Evelyn.

"No, he isn't." She laughed. "He usually doesn't use his claws and teeth. I wouldn't put my face too close to him, though. She picked Sugar up. The cat nuzzled her face and licked her chin. "He lets me do this. Nobody else should trust him."

"How old is he? He looks pretty young."

"He's about three and a half months old now. They grow up really fast. I have to say kittens are really cute and fun to watch. However, I won't mind it when he becomes a lazy grown cat."

"I know what you mean. My mom always had cats."

"So, are you avoiding talking to me about something? You said you had something to say."

"I think it's more like stalling than avoiding. It's about your sister."

"Are you going to break up with her? She seems to think things are going well between you."

"No. I'm head over heels in love with her. I can't think of anything else."

"I hope it isn't distracting you from your work and your studies."

"It was for a while. That's when I realized I was going to have to have some discipline. I was spending every evening at the restaurant just so I could look at her. I'd wake up so tired in the morning it was hard to work. I even got behind in one of my graduate classes. I had to struggle to catch up, so I made a rule. I can go to the café one night a week. Only for as long as it takes me to eat. We usually spend her evening off together. Half a day on Sunday so I can study half a day."

"It's still a lot of time. I miss her. We usually spent Sundays together before you came along."

"I'm sorry about that. But I'm not going to change it. That's what I came to talk about. I'm want to ask her to marry me."

Evelyn's mouth dropped open. She gaped at him for a second then snapped it shut. "Darren, that's a little fast don't you think? You've only been seeing each other for a little while."

"I know it's right. I think Alice does, too, but you're right. I need to give it a little more time. Not to be sure, I'm already sure. It's just a little soon. I don't want to rush things. I still need to establish myself at my job. I haven't worked there that long.

"Why are you telling me now if it's too soon?"

"Because you're her twin. I've heard about the twin connection thing. I thought you should have some time to get used to it. I can see the truth in the rumor. You guys are really close."

"I couldn't live without her. That's thoughtful. I appreciate it. One of the things about twins is that they have a hard time keeping things from each other. I don't know how long I can keep this."

"I'm going to talk to her about it. I mean, no ring, no down on one knee at this point. But just let her know the way my thoughts are going. Maybe she doesn't feel the same way." He sipped his coffee and looked out the window. "That would kill me."

"What would you do?"

"I'd have to get to work convincing her." He smiled. Evelyn felt warmed by how happy he looked. He really loved her sister. Sadly, she thought, I can relate.

"When will you talk to her about it?"

"We're having lunch tomorrow. I'll bring it up then. Listen, Ev, we're going out to your parents' house on Sunday. Alice wants me to ride the horses with her." He shivered. "That'll be a good laugh. I've never been on a horse."

"It's not that hard. Dapple and Roan are good horses. You won't have to handle them. They'll handle themselves."

"It'll be the first time I meet your parents. I was wondering if you would go out there, too. I'm a little nervous. Another familiar face would be nice."

"There are only two rideable horses. I don't know. I'm not sure it's my place in a situation like this."

"Of course, it's your place. You're twins. You don't need to ride with us. Just come for dinner. It's an afternoon picnic if it isn't too cold. Your mom is going to make potato salad. Your dad is going to grill ribs."

"I don't know if I can resist that. Okay, I'll come. I haven't been out to see Mom lately. She's been having sort of a rough time."

"Alice told me. Good, I'm glad you're coming." He stood up and took his jacket off the coat rack. "I think I'll go on over to the café now. I can't wait to set my eyes on her." He smiled stupidly. "You look just like her. That makes you beautiful, too. But I can tell the difference." He waved and went out the door.

The cat jumped up to the bar again. "Funny, Sugar. Jamie can tell the difference, too. Nobody else can. Even Dad can't at a glance, sometimes not even Mom. Do you think that means something?"

*

On Saturday before the lunch rush, Alice went to the nursery to look for Evelyn. She found her unloading supplies in the shop. "What's this thing for?" She picked up a gardening tool from the box of supplies that Evelyn was unloading. It had a handle and a long metal rod that was bent in the middle. At the end of the rod were two prongs with something like pegs on each end. "These pegs on the end are blunt so I doubt you could use it to move the soil or anything."

Evelyn looked over at Alice. "I've never been able to figure it out. They just send us a few with every load, a freebee I guess. I put them out on the shelf in the hopes that a customer will come along and explain it to me."

"Imagine that, something you don't know about gardening."

"Is there something you want, Alice? I need to go out to the greenhouse. I know you won't want to follow me out there. I'll be fertilizing. We got in a new shipment of cow manure. Your delicate sense of smell won't tolerate it."

"My sense of smell isn't that delicate. I just want to spend some time with my Sissy."

"You only call me Sissy when you want something."

"You have become very cynical, Sissy." Alice followed her out the door. She shivered when they hit the cold outside air. "Winter is coming."

"Maybe you should go get a sweater. It is cold out here."

"It won't be in the greenhouse." She opened the door and held it for Evelyn.

"Okay, what's going on? Has Jamie been lured here by some trick? Are you going to go back inside and lock us in here together or something?"

"God, Ev, you're getting paranoid. I just wanted to spend some time with you. We haven't spent much time together lately. You're working so hard here. I'm spending all my spare time with Darren." She smiled wistfully.

"So that's going well?"

"It is. I know I've said this before but I think he's the one."

"You may have said it once or twice." Evelyn laughed. "But I believe you every time."

"We had lunch together the other day."

Evelyn stifled the urge to say, 'I know.'

"Ev, he's talking about marriage."

"I know." She cringed but it was too late.

"What do you mean you know?"

"He came over to my house the other night before he went to the café to have dinner. He wanted to talk to me about it."

"I think he's a little confused. It's the father he's supposed to get permission from." Evelyn looked at Alice quickly. She sounded so angry.

"Don't be mad, Al. He's worried because we're so close."

"Don't you think he should have talked to me about it first?" Alice's face was set in angry lines. She crossed her arms in a defensive gesture.

"Maybe he should have, but this is new ground for him, for all of us. Try to forgive him if it bothers you. He's only thinking of us. That's nice, a lot of men wouldn't."

Alice relaxed her face and dropped her arms. "I guess you're right. See," she laughed. "I *must* be in love. I can get so mad at him sometimes. I can't *stay* mad for more than a few seconds."

"So, you're not unhappy about the marriage talk?"

"I was startled at first. We haven't been seeing each other for long. Ev, we talk so easily. I think we already know each other pretty well." She sighed.

Evelyn rolled her eyes and looked around the greenhouse. "Where did the guys put that fertilizer?"

"Follow your nose, or don't you smell that stuff anymore?" Alice nodded toward the far corner where a garden cart stood with two mesh bags of manure in it.

"Good, now are you going to hang out while I spread it on the bulbs I'm forcing for the new year?"

"Sure, I have a few more minutes before the lunch rush. I was wondering if you'd come to Mom and Dad's on Sunday. We're going out to ride and for an afternoon barbecue. It's the first time he'll meet them. I think having you there would ease some of the tension."

Evelyn looked at her and Alice stopped short. "Don't tell me. He already asked you to come." She crossed her arms again.

"Yes, but don't be mad at him. This is new ground for all of us, remember?"

She dropped her arms again and smiled. "You're right. So, you'll be there."

"Yeah, I feel a little strange being the fifth wheel, but I'll be there. I need to visit Mom anyway." She shrugged and went to the cart. "Oh no!" She jumped back.

"What?" Alice hurried over to see what Evelyn was looking at. In the cart tangled hopelessly in the mesh bag was a writhing snake. They both stood and stared for a few seconds.

"Do you know what kind of snake that is?" Alice asked.

"Yeah, it's a copper head."

"I was afraid of that. Shouldn't he be sleeping at this time of year?"

"Yes, they're cold blooded, but the manure is warm. I suppose he got rousted or something and went toward the warmth."

"What are we going to do?" Alice asked. Neither one of them had moved. "Should I go and get someone, one of the boys or Darcy?"

"No, they'll just kill him."

"I don't want to kill him, Ev. But what else can we do? He's stuck in the mesh. It's just around his middle part. His head is free and clear. He'll bite us if we try to free him."

"Wait a minute. Stay here, Al. Don't go anywhere. I'll need your help."

"Help to do what?"

"You'll see. Just don't go anywhere." Evelyn hurried from the greenhouse.

Alice stood perfectly still staring at the writhing creature. "I'm not sure I want to stay but I can't seem to move."

Evelyn was back in a matter of minutes. In one hand, she carried the unidentified garden tool and a pair of scissors. In the other hand, she had a plastic terrarium.

"I think I just figured out what this tool is for." She handed the scissors and the terrarium to Alice. "Now, I'll trap his head with these prongs. You cut the mesh off him."

"How about *I* trap his head and *you* cut the mesh."

"I don't know. I think you can trust me not to panic and let him go better than I can trust you."

"I don't like it." Alice sighed. "But I think you might be right. Okay, let's get this done. What am I going to do with the terrarium?"

"After we free him you'll scoop him into the terrarium, then I'll release his head after he's inside. You'll have to close the lid fast so he doesn't get back out."

Evelyn managed to trap the snake's head after a few tries and Alice cut the mesh loose. Together they managed to scoop the snake into the terrarium and close it tightly."

"Let me tape the top closed," Evelyn said and hurried to the work table to get some tape.

"Now what do we do with him?" Alice asked.

"I don't know. I'll call Dad. He'll tell us what to do."

"Here." Alice handed her the terrarium "I need to go on back to work. It was nice to spend some time with you, Ev." She laughed. "What do you have planned for next time?"

*

Sunday was a beautiful fall day. It was cool but not cold. The air was still. The wind that had brought the cooler weather last week had died down. The sun was shining. Evelyn smiled when she pulled into the drive at her parents' house. She'd arrived just in time to see Alice and Darren riding up the hill toward the trail. Darren was clinging to the saddle horn and Alice was talking, teaching, surely.

"He doesn't look too steady," she said to Jeff as she got out of the car.

"Worse than Jamie even. I made her take her cell phone in case of an accident."

"I'm sure they'll be okay. Roan is a sweetheart." She wrapped her arms around her dad's waist and hugged him.

"What a nice greeting." He hugged her back and kissed the top of her head. "We just saw each other yesterday."

"I know. I was just thinking how happy I am that you didn't let those people adopt Dapple."

"Well, I want them to stay together." He turned to go into the house. "Not to mention that you girls want them," he muttered.

Evelyn smiled and followed him inside. "Where's Mom?"

"She's in the back yard with Albert." They went through the kitchen to the back yard. Amanda sat in a chair feeding the tiny kitten from the bottle and smiling. There was a cage with toys and a bed sitting on the deck beside her. The kitten was wrapped up in a blanket.

Evelyn smiled. Her mother looked happy for a change. She felt a warmth spread through her and made a mental note to thank Jamie again the next time she saw him. If there was a next time. "Hey, Mom." She kissed her mother on the head and looked down at the little bundle. "He's grown and his eyes are open."

"I can't believe how fast kittens grow," Amanda said. "We figure he's about three weeks old now. His vision is still not very good. He's at least seeing light and dark and movement I think."

"You don't think it's too cool out here for him?"

"Not right now. The sun is shining and the wind isn't blowing. Plus," she moved the blanket aside. "I have him on a heating pad. I'll put him in the cage when he finishes eating. I worry about hawks."

Evelyn looked toward the sky. "I hadn't even thought about that. What a terrible thought."

"We're not going to let it happen." Amanda rose from the chair and nestled the now sleeping kitten into the cage. "Now." She turned to Evelyn and wrapped her arms around her. "I can give you a proper greeting. Jeff, go in and get the lemonade, please. And bring out the new blue bubble glasses and some ice. Let's sit down. You can tell me about what you're doing. Dad says you're giving the business a whole new outlook."

Evelyn could only gape at her mother. Things had really improved. She looked down at the little lump in the blanket in the cage. Thanks, Albert, she thought. Thanks Jamie.

It was probably an hour later that Alice and Darren came back. Daren looked a little pale, but sat down and took the beer that Jeff offered him. He opened the bottle and took a drink. His hands shook, but he smiled.

"How did you like the ride, Darren?" Jeff's smile was more of a smirk.

"It was nice." Darren's hand was steadying a little bit. He laughed. "Actually, I wasn't that crazy about it. I mean the path is great. The countryside is beautiful, but I think I'd rather have been on a mountain bike."

Alice stood next to his chair. She laughed and ran a hand through his hair. "Honesty is always the best policy." She turned to her family. "I was thinking I would have to call you to come and get him, Dad. Horseback riding is not my Darren's thing."

"That's okay." Jeff laughed. "Mountain biking is fun, too."

*

Jamie pulled into the drive at the Landrum's house. He'd been at a friend's house a little further up the road. He thought he'd stop and check in on Albert on his way home. He stopped when he saw both Alice and Evelyn's cars there. Maybe not, he thought, and pulled back out of the driveway. The car backfired, sputtered, moved forward when he pressed on the gas, then died.

"Oh man! I swear I heard the thing groan." He got out of the car and opened the hood. "I don't think there's anything I can do about this." He looked back toward the house. "Oh no." Jeff, Alice, and some man he didn't know were walking up the driveway toward him. He ran his hand through his hair and looked at the sky.

"What's the problem, Jamie?" Jeff went around and looked under the hood. "What isn't the problem is a little more like it." He laughed. "Lucky thing you were here when it happened and not down the road a mile."

"Yeah, lucky," he muttered. "I was visiting a friend up the road. I thought I'd stop and check on Albert and Red and Sterling. When I saw that you had company I was just going to go on. I didn't mean to disturb you."

Jeff looked back at his daughter's cars then at Darren. "Oh, yes, company. This is Darren Drake. He's with Alice. Darren this is James Parnell." He looked back at Jamie and noticed the blush rising up his neck to his face. Poor kid. "Alice, get behind the wheel of the car and let's push it to the side of the road. Then come on down. We'll call a tow truck."

"Thanks, I appreciate the push, but don't worry about the tow truck. I have Triple A. I'll just call on my cell and wait up here for them."

"Nonsense, come on down and have a beer while you wait. You can get a look at the cats. I'm sure it'll take Triple A a while to get out here."

They pushed the car to the side of the road and Alice got out. "Come on, Jamie. Come back to the house. Evelyn won't bite you. She *will* think we set this up, though, Dad."

"Well, we didn't. Listen Jamie, I'm sorry about that last stunt."

Darren scratched his head. "What are you talking about?"

"I'll tell you about it later, Darren." Alice took his arm. "Let's go back down."

Tension mounted in the little group as they approached the house. Evelyn and Amanda stood on the front stoop with their arms crossed and their faces set.

"It's not a set up," Alice said before they could say a word.

"No, it isn't!" Jeff said. "I mean how could we arrange for James Jr.'s car to break down in front of the house."

"It really isn't, Ev." Jamie stepped forward. "Mrs. Landrum, I was visiting a friend up the road and thought I'd have a look at the cats on my way home. When I saw you had company I tried to leave." He looked back up the drive, disgusted. "The damn car chose that minute to die." He quickly looked back at her. "I'm sorry, Mrs. Landrum. I didn't mean to swear."

Amanda's expression softened. "It's okay, Jamie. I can stand a swear." She looked seriously again at Jeff and Alice. "I know Jamie is innocent in this. I'm still not sure about the two of you."

"I swear, Mom." Alice stood half behind Darren. "You scared us enough the last time."

"Well." She looked at Jeff. "We'll talk about it later. Come on in and join us, Jamie. Albert is in the living room." She turned and went inside. Alice and Jeff and Darren followed her inside.

"What's going on?" Darren whispered to Alice as they went by.

"I'll explain it later."

Evelyn relaxed her arms and smiled at Jamie. "I'm sorry. How did they get you to come out here?"

"They didn't. Really, Ev. It's just bad luck."

"Oh, I don't know if it's so bad. Come on in and see Albert. You won't believe how much he's grown." She took his hand and pulled him through the door.

"You've done a wonderful job with him, Mrs. Landrum."

"Thanks, Jamie. I've loved every minute of it. Will you stay to dinner? Triple A can tow your car to the shop and leave it there. You can't do anything about it until tomorrow anyway."

"Thanks, but I'd better ride with them." He snuggled the kitten to his face.

"Stay for dinner. Please. One of the girls can take you home."

"I brought Darren," Alice said. "And my car only seats two. Evelyn would have to do it."

The tension in the room was growing. Darren shifted uncomfortably.

"No. Thank you, really," Jamie said. "I'll ride with triple A. Marisa can give me a ride home. I'd like to go see the barn cats while I wait though, if that's okay."

"Of course."

Jamie turned toward the kitchen to go out the back door.

"Wait, Jamie, I'll come with you," Evelyn said. She winced at the panic written on his face when he turned back. "Darren, why don't you come along?" She looked back at her family. "I think Mom wants a word with Dad and Alice."

The relief on Jamie's face made Evelyn's heart sink. *He doesn't want to be alone with me. He really doesn't love me anymore.*

*

"So, are you going to tell me what that was about?" Darren asked on the ride home.

"It's kind of a long story."

"It's kind of a long ride."

Alice took a deep breath. "Evelyn and Jamie were sweethearts when she was in high school. He's older, so he was already out on his own. They were seriously in love. After she went away to school things stopped. Ev can't understand why. When she first came back she tried to talk to him about it, he just avoided her. He's still avoiding her. I think he feels like he's not good enough for her."

"Well, that's just stupid. They're obviously still in love."

She looked at him and smiled. "I love you, Darren. You're so perceptive."

He smiled back and stroked her cheek.

"Well, anyway, you shouldn't say the word stupid when you're talking about Jamie. Because that's his problem. He thinks he's stupid. He had some learning disabilities growing up. I guess he still has them. He has a hard time with tests and all. He can't do well enough on the boards to get into graduate school. Then he made a mess for himself buying some land. He was going to turn it into an animal rescue, but he just doesn't make enough money."

"I'd think he could borrow the money for that. It is a small business even if it's non-profit."

"He tried. He couldn't write the prospectus. Dad and David worked on it with him and it finally came through. I think Jamie feels a little humbled because he needed help."

"Well, that's just stup...... I forgot. Don't use that word." He laughed. "Well, I really liked Jamie. We've got to get them back together."

"Be careful, sweetheart. Dad and I made a very clumsy attempt. Mom nearly killed us. I wouldn't want her to be mad at you, too."

"I'm not as clumsy as you. Is that what she wanted to talk to you and your dad about tonight?"

"Yes, I think we convinced her it really wasn't a set up. Unless God set it up."

"Jamie and I made a date to play tennis next Thursday. Maybe I can think of something by then.

"Like I said, be careful. Oh, and just for your information, Jamie will smear you into the ground in tennis."

"Hey, I'm pretty good."

"Did he tell you he's a pro?"

"Yeah, I'm prepared to get smeared into the ground. Maybe I can learn something."

Chapter 10

"Ruth, it's beautiful!" Evelyn stood in the center of the waiting room. "The color is fantastic. What did you say the name of it was?"

"Potentially Purple."

"I think I'll paint my bedroom that color. I love vivid colors."

"You don't think this is too vivid, do you? With purple, you have to be careful. There's a fine line between pretty and psychedelic."

Evelyn laughed. "I know what you mean, but no, a black light would do nothing to this color." She turned a slow circle looking at the room. "Your pictures are great, very serene, calming, exactly what you want in a doctor's waiting room." She smiled at Ruth. "I have another client who's interested in an interior decorator. What do you think?"

Ruth sat down in one of the chairs. "I haven't finished this yet. I have some new furniture coming and this stuff," She patted the chair next to her. "has to go out for re-upholstery. Honestly, I'm tired." She rubbed her face. "And I miss Bradley."

"Oh." Evelyn sat down beside her. "I'm sorry. I hadn't thought about that. It's funny, I thought it would be such a relief for you to have some time away from him. You know what? I'll miss him if he stops coming to the nursery."

"Oh, don't worry about that. I don't think I could keep him away from there if I tried." She looked at her watch. "Speaking of Bradley, I have to pick him up at his homeschool group. He has his first tennis lesson with Jamie in an hour and a half. He'll need to get changed."

"Do you want me to tell my client you're not interested?" They stood and walked to the door.

"No, I'd like to meet with them. I'm thinking if I gave myself more time. You know, if I didn't commit to such a short period of time to get the job done. Maybe I wouldn't have to be away from him so much. I'll have to charge more, too. This job proved that I can do this, but I barely broke even. If I'd had to pay for daycare I wouldn't have broken even."

"Absolutely, charge more and take more time."

"I might get outbid that way, but it's the only way I can keep doing this. I did enjoy it. Let me meet with the client, see the space, then we'll see what happens."

"Okay. I'll have them call you."

*

Evelyn sat on a stool in the Wild Bird section of the nursery. It was actually set aside from the nursery in such a way that it was almost like its own shop. That was good because her Uncle Brian needed a project of his own. He'd been so lonely and sad for the year since David's mom had died.

"So, how's business, Uncle Brian?"

"It's okay. Starting a little slow, but breaking even at least. I need to get some marketing going. David is working on that. You know he majored in marketing in college. Problem is he doesn't have a lot of spare time with the café, and he's trying to spend a little more time at home."

"We have a marketing group. Have you talked to them?"

"No, it's kind of awkward. I don't want David to think I don't have faith in him, but he really doesn't have time."

"David won't mind. Just tell him. He'll understand." She turned on the stool when she heard her name called.

"Ev! Ev!" Bradley was racing across the room toward her. "Look at my racket!" He swung it dangerously close the the display of tropical plants in the middle of the nursery and actually hit the display of wind chimes as he came into the wild bird section. The resulting chimes made conversation impossible. "Sorry," he said when the sound died down.

"No harm done." Evelyn took the racket and turned it in her hand. "It's beautiful! How did the first lesson go?"

"Great! I think I'm a natural."

"And modest, too." She laughed.

Ruth came a little more slowly to where they stood. Darren was with her.

"You should have seen him, Evelyn," he said. "He is a natural. Jamie and I played before he got there. When I saw that Bradley's lesson was next I stayed to watch. I was very impressed."

"I suppose Jamie smeared you into the ground."

Darren looked at his feet. "Yeah, but he said I was the best competition he'd had since he stopped competing. I think he was just being nice."

"Will you play with him again?"

"You bet, we're going to play on Thursday. Coincidentally, so is Bradley. Why don't you come and watch? I won't be that much fun to watch, but Bradley will."

"You know, Darren," Bradley spoke seriously. "I prefer to be called Brad. I don't like the l-e-y."

"Oh. Sorry."

"So, will you come, Ev?" Bradley asked. "I want you to see how good I am."

"Like I said, Brad, modesty becomes you."

Ruth laughed. "I think I can see his head swelling."

Bradley put both hands on his head. "It is not. Will you come, Ev?"

"I don't know, Brad. Thursday's are busy days around here. A number of the shipments come in. I don't know if I can get away."

Bradley's bottom lip began to quiver. "You don't care! You just don't care!"

"Brad, I do too care, but I care about my work, too."

"Oh, you just think they can't do without you here. You're not so great!"

Darcy approached the group. "What's going on. I can hear you yelling from my office."

"Ev thinks you can't do without her for a few hours. Talk about a swollen head!" Bradley burst into tears. He grabbed the racket out of her hand and ran toward the bathroom. "I hate you! You just don't care!"

"There he goes," Ruth said, "Acting like a four-year-old."

"It always startles me when that happens. But I guess he is a four-year-old."

"A very tired one. It's been a long day with the home school group and the tennis lesson. He was so excited last night he couldn't get to sleep. I'll give him a minute to calm down and go after him."

"We can handle Thursday, Evelyn," Darcy said. "You can go watch him play tennis."

"I thought you were taking Thursday and Friday off."

"I am, but your dad will be here. He can supervise."

"Is that okay, Ruth? I hate to give in to his tantrum."

"We won't talk about it. Why don't you plan to come and surprise him? He really does want you to see him play. He's grown very fond of you. I would be jealous if I was the jealous type." She laughed.

"Nobody can take the place of Mom. Okay I'll come."

"Come a little early, Evelyn. You'll really enjoy seeing me get smeared into the ground." Darren said and turned to go. "See ya ..." he waved as he headed up the stairs to the café.

*

Evelyn sailed along in her car toward her family home in the country. She was going to visit her mother. She hadn't been out by herself for a while and just felt the need to spend some one on one time with Amanda. She had the top down in her car. The heat was pumping and she was bundled up against the cold. They were going into November and the fall was gradually fading into winter. But she just wanted to feel the cool air blowing on her face.

She pulled into the driveway and got out of her car. Elmo was in the pasture grazing. He looked up at her, twitched his ear as if to wave to her then lowered his head back to the grass. He looked bored, she thought. Sweetie was nowhere in sight. Maybe it wasn't working out.

The kitchen door was unlocked so she went inside unannounced. Not that they ever had to announce themselves. "Mom," she called and went through to the living room. "Mom, where are you?"

"I'm up here, honey, in the exercise room."

Things must be getting better. Jeff had said she'd quit exercising. You really knew she was depressed when she didn't exercise. Evelyn hurried up the stairs to the exercise room. Her parents had invested in a full gym in the loft over the garage. Her dad had always said he'd rather have the equipment himself than spend the money on a club where you were only renting someone else's.

"I'm almost finished," Amanda said. She was on the treadmill. She was moving at a sedate pace. Evelyn knew that meant she was either warming up or cooling down. She had strict rules about her exercise.

"You must be feeling better. You're working out."

"Feeling better than what?" Amanda didn't like to talk about her feelings much.

"Come on, Mom. You know you had us all worried."

"I guess so. I'm sorry." She stepped off the tread mill and picked up a towel to wipe the sweat off her face. "I do feel better. I hate to admit it, but I think it's that little cat that did it. Sometimes I get sad when I remember that he'll grow old and die, just like the rest of them."

"That's a long way off. Think of all the joy he'll bring you until then."

"That's what I try to do, or just stop thinking about it at all." She picked up her water and drank. "I introduced him to LuLu the other day. You know she's always wanted a baby of her own. I think she was hoping for a puppy, but a kitten seems to be alright with her."

"Mom, she's a Rottweiler. I know she's a sweet one, but remember how she babied her toys? She'd put them between her front paws and growl at anyone that came close. Then she'd rip the insides out of them. You'd better be careful with Albert."

"I watch pretty closely. But I think she knows the difference between real flesh and bones and a stuffed toy. She was so cute growling at Arthur whenever he came around to sniff. He pouted. I think he had his feelings hurt."

Evelyn laughed. Amanda's face was glowing while she talked about her pets.

"Honey." Amanda put her hand on Evelyn's forehead. "You're all flushed. Are you sick?"

"No." She laughed and stood to take off her jacket and hat. "I came out with the heater on in my car and the top down. It's just such a beautiful day. The air is so nice out here. I wanted to feel the wind on my face."

"That's probably not the smartest thing to do, but I can see the appeal." Evelyn followed her as she went down the stairs to the kitchen. Amanda filled the kettle with water and put it on to boil for tea. "So why are you here? Your dad is at the shop today."

"I came to see you. We haven't spent much time together lately. I've been so busy. When we do see each other it's with everyone else. I felt like I wanted some one on one time."

"Well, good. I'm glad you still feel that way sometimes, but usually when you do it means something's bothering you."

"We have fun together, too."

"Yes, we do. You're more like me than Alice is. She's more like your dad with his outgoing personality."

"I'm more like him professionally, but it's true. They like to be in the spotlight. I prefer to stay in the shadows." Without warning her eyes filled with tears. She sniffed hoping to clear them. It didn't work.

Amanda crossed the room and wrapped her arms around her daughter. She just held her, didn't say anything. Evelyn rested her head on her mother's shoulder and let the tears flow. They stayed like that, silent, swaying only a little in comfort. She could remember this all her life, her mother's quiet comfort whenever things were hard. She sniffed and pulled gently away to get a tissue. Then kissed her mother on the cheek.

"You want to talk about it?" Amanda took the whistling kettle off the burner and poured the boiling water into the teapot.

"I wouldn't know what to talk about. I didn't even know I was going to cry until it happened."

"We'll let that steep a minute." She put the teapot in the middle of the table and got down two cups. "Why do you think you cried?"

"Well, I guess it's Jamie. I've been working so hard since I got back and started in the business. Uncle Brian's wild bird section is up and running. He's not happy with the way it's going, but that's just a matter of marketing. We hire people to do that for us. I just have to convince him to work with them. Darcy has pretty much quit being a butthead." She looked up quickly at her mother. "I'm sorry. I shouldn't have put it that way."

"No, you shouldn't have, but I'll have to agree with you that she was acting like a butthead." Their laughter released some of the tension Evelyn was feeling.

"The corporate business is going well. Ruth doesn't know if she wants to work with me on the decorating end of it. I'll be disappointed about that. She's become a friend. She can still be a friend. I just think we'd make good business partners, too."

"Well, I'm sorry she might not work with you, but it actually sounds like things are going pretty well. What's making you sad?" She reached across the table and brushed a tear off Evelyn's cheek.

"I go home at night and all there is, is Sugar." The tears started again. She dropped her face into her hands. "He's wonderful. I love him so much. But, it's not enough, Mom. Alice is so busy with Darren. I can't even hang out with her on her nights off." She wiped her eyes and picked up the tea her mother had poured for her.

"You miss Jamie. It couldn't just be anyone to spend time with. You miss Jamie."

"Yeah." She sniffed and took a tea cake from the tray Amanda had set out. "I was so sure I could just learn to live without him, but I can't. All this plotting and scheming everyone is doing only makes things worse."

"Honey, do you think he still has feelings for you?"

She looked into her tea cup and swirled the liquid around for a few seconds. "Yes. Yes, I do. He has some idea that he's not good enough for me. Or something like that. I can't get through to him."

"He always was hard headed."

"Yeah." Evelyn laughed.

"Your dad and your sister aren't plotting again, are they?"

"I don't think so, but it seems to be a contagious disease. It seems like everyone is. Or maybe I'm just getting paranoid."

A tiny mewing sound came from the corner of the room. Amanda stood up and went to the plastic carrier.

"Look at Albert," Evelyn exclaimed. "Mom, he's grown so much. He's up on all fours now."

"Here hold him while I warm his bottle." She handed the kitten to Evelyn.

Evelyn rubbed his little head on her cheek. "He's so precious. No wonder you feel better, Mom."

"I think he's almost ready to graduate from a carrier to a crate. I just have to make sure he can't get through the bars. I may start introducing solid food to him, too. You know Evelyn, Jamie says that bottle fed kittens tend to grow up to be bad cats. He says he thinks it might be because they didn't have siblings. I was thinking getting him together with Sugar might be a good way to work on that."

"Oh, I don't know, Mom. Sugar is already a bad cat, and *he* had siblings." She laughed.

"Well, I think we should try. Not yet, he's too small, but when he gets more solid on his feet I'd like to bring him over to your apartment to play. Would you mind if we at least tried?"

"Of course not, but be forewarned. Sugar is a terror." She was surprised her mother wanted to come into the city. She hadn't wanted to in ages. She only went into the city when she had to for some reason.

"We'll manage. If it doesn't work we can put Albert in his carrier and put him in the bedroom while we go to lunch. I'd like to go to Alice's Café. I haven't been there since it opened. Your dad has tried to get me to go, but well ..."

"I know." Evelyn stroked the kitten that was sucking loudly on his bottle in her mother's hands. "I think that would be fun. You think in another week, he'll be ready?"

"Yes, I do. Let's make it Friday. That's your day off, isn't it? Maybe we can even do some shopping. I need some clothes. I'm starting to look dumpy. Your dad doesn't like it when I look dumpy. He says I'm hiding from him under my clothes."

Evelyn could feel a weight lifting from her chest. Mom was going to be okay.

"Honey, about Jamie ..."

"It's okay, Mom." Evelyn stood to put on her coat. "I've got to work this out myself. There isn't anything you can do but be a shoulder to cry on."

"You know I'll always be that."

"Thanks, Mom." She bent to kiss her on the cheek. "I love you."

*

Evelyn pulled into the parking lot of the public tennis court Jamie was using for non-country club lessons. She got out of the car and looked around for Darren. He wasn't there. She looked around the parking lot for his car. She was pretty sure she could recognize it. It wasn't there.

"Hey, Ev." She looked up at the sound of Jamie's voice. He was approaching holding his racket by his side. He looked so nice to her. He wore his sweat pants and shirt so well. His arms were so muscular, the right one slightly larger than the left. And his hands were beautiful. She caught herself staring at them and took a deep breath to calm her thumping heart.

"Where's Darren?" She asked noticing that Jamie had a sheepish look on his face.

"He cancelled. I tried to call you, but I guess you didn't have your cell phone with you. You should really work on that, Ev. Suppose you had an accident and needed help. You are a little clumsy. It's not beyond the realm of possibility." He laughed.

"Another set up," she said.

"Guess so. We might as well sit down and wait for Brad." He took her arm and guided her to a bench. Her skin tingled where he touched her. She laughed at herself. Being a little dramatic, she thought.

"What are you laughing about?"

"What?" She looked up at Jamie's question. "Oh, just all these silly games our friends are playing."

"Hmmm." They sat in silence for a minute.

"I'm glad I only came a little early. We won't have long to wait."

"No. How's the job going, Ev? I haven't even asked. You must be really happy. You've worked for this all your life."

"Yeah, I have." She smiled up at him. "At first it was scary. The reality just didn't measure up to the dream. Darcy was so nasty. We had it out. It turns out she was afraid I wanted her job."

"That's dumb," Jamie said. "You don't want her job. You want your dad's."

"That's what I told her." They laughed. An awkward silence followed.

"How's the rescue coming along?"

"Got a long way to go, but thanks to your dad and David, we're seeing progress."

There was another silence.

"Jamie, listen." Evelyn reached for his hand. He didn't pull it away.

"You came! You came!" Bradley jumped up and down waving his racket as he ran across the parking lot. Ruth followed close behind reaching for him in vain.

"Bradley, I've told you again and again not to run through a parking lot. You're too small for people to see you behind their cars."

"That's right, Brad." Evelyn got up and accepted the hug that Bradley demanded.

"I'm sorry." He was so excited that his apology didn't sound very sincere. "Come on Jamie! Let's show her how good I am."

"There's that modesty again." Ruth and Evelyn laughed as Jamie and Bradley moved onto the court."

"Wow, he is good." Evelyn said at the end of the session. They had watched in relative silence. It was almost unreal seeing a four-year-old play tennis like a pro. "It's hard to believe he's four years old."

"It is. That can be a problem. I never should have let him get out of that car by himself. I'm still shaking at the thought of what could have happened." Ruth clasped her hands in her lap. "But after the discussion about the Second World War we had on the way over, in which I was completely ignorant, I guess I just forgot. Scares me to death."

"Well, it all turned out okay, so try to calm down. Your hands are shaking."

They looked at the court where Jamie and Bradley were picking up balls.

"Jamie makes him help with the balls. He told him he'd had enough of spoiled little rich kids at the country club. Bradley pitched a fit last week. Remember how tired he was? But Jamie didn't let him off the hook. He's good with kids."

"Yeah, he is." Evelyn looked down at the ground. She suddenly felt sad.

"Did you see how good I was?!" Bradley rushed up to them waving his racket again.

"Hey!" Evelyn grabbed it just before it hit her in the face. "Be careful with that thing."

"I'll be better than Jamie next week."

"I think it'll take a little longer than that, buddy." Jamie ruffled Bradley's hair.

"I hate when you do that." Brad brushed at his hair to get it back in place.

"That's why I do it." Jamie ruffled the hair that Bradley had just smoothed down. The child laughed and smoothed his hair again. Evelyn watched the scene. The look on Jamie's face was more relaxed and happy than she'd seen him in a long time.

"You know, he really could go pro," he said to Ruth. "Of course, I'm sure he'll have a lot more important things to do. This kid could do anything he wanted."

"Having too many choices can be as big a problem as not having enough." Ruth looked at Bradley. She was worried, Evelyn noted. She still hadn't gotten over the scare in the parking lot.

"Jamie." Bradley tugged on his hand and looked up at him. "Will you take me out to your rescue place? I've been asking Ev, but she's always too busy."

"Brad, you always ask me when I'm at work." Evelyn laughed.

"We'll see, kid. I'm afraid I'm pretty busy right now. My schedule at the school is pretty full and with the lessons on the side, well, we'll see when I can fit it in."

"Everyone is always so busy." Bradley stuck out his lower lip and pouted for a minute. You could see from the expression on his face he'd had an idea. "I was thinking of being a vet when I grow up. How will I know if I like animals if I don't ever get to see any?"

"I thought you were going to be a horticulturist," Evelyn said.

"I thought you were going to be a tennis pro." Jamie tapped him on the head with his racket.

"I'm making a list. I'll need to investigate the veterinary field."

"That was a good one, Bradley." Ruth took his hand. He pouted again at being figured out. "Come on let's go. Daddy will be home soon and I haven't started dinner." She looked at Evelyn. "I'll need to talk to you about the new job. I think I'll take it if they're okay with my quote. But there will be some restrictions. We'll talk later when we have time." She guided Bradley across the parking lot.

Evelyn smiled and looked back at Jamie.

"That's some kid," he said and started to gather his tennis equipment.

"He is. I'm madly in love with him." She cringed at the statement. "Listen, Jamie ..."

"I've got to go, Ev." He turned and carried his stuff to his car.

"You mean you got the thing going again?" She called after him.

He turned around and laughed. "Yeah, amazing, huh."

She felt a lump in her throat and turned toward her own car. She heard the backfire as he started his wreck and drove out.

"Looks like Darren's set up didn't work any better than the others." She hung her head and walked to her car.

*

She didn't sleep well that night. She kept looking at the clock, then she would worry about how tired she was going to be at work the next day. And of all days, she was opening. She didn't usually open on Saturday, but Darcy had taken a long weekend. She was finally starting to let Evelyn take some of the pressure off her.

At about 4:00am Sugar got up on the bed and curled up next to her face. He put his paw on her cheek and started to purr.

"I love you, Sugar." She kissed him on his soft head. "You'll never stop loving me will you." She snuggled close to him and finally drifted off to sleep.

The morning came much too fast. She dragged herself out of bed and took a cool shower to try to jolt her system. It didn't work. She went to the kitchen after she was dressed, opened the refrigerator, then realized that she had no appetite. She gathered her things and went outside to walk to work. She passed her car and stopped, pondered it for a minute, then got in and drove the two minutes it took to get to the nursery.

The morning dragged by. She watched the clock just like she had the night before knowing that it would only make things worse. One of the cashiers had called in sick so she had to work check out. She just hoped she wouldn't screw up the money too much. A shipment of stones came in. She had to divide her time between the shop and the loading dock. When the second shift arrived at 11:30 she went to her office. She looked at the chair behind the desk and went to the easy chair she'd put in for short rest stops during the day. She put her head on the cushioned back and closed her eyes. Maybe a short power nap would help.

"God! Ev. Are you alright?" Alice stood in the doorway. "Are you sick? You look terrible."

"Thanks, Al. You can always cheer me up." She stood up, walked to the desk chair and plopped down hard. She didn't even have the strength to sit. She put her head down on the desk. "I'm not sick. I just couldn't get to sleep last night. I finally did at about 4:00. At least that's the last time I looked at the clock. Sugar purred me to sleep. At least he still loves me."

"I take it Darren's little trick didn't work."

"It's a losing battle, Al. Give up. I have."

"It's beginning to look like you're right. I'm sorry. I told him not to do it, but I guess I didn't discourage him very hard."

"It's okay." She stood. "Listen, it's about lunch time. I'm going home to see if I can sleep for half an hour or forty-five minutes. Can I tell the staff to check with you if there's any problem? You wouldn't have to get your hands dirty, maybe just make a decision or two."

"Sure, why don't you take the rest of the day. You really look tired."

"I can't. Darcy's off. Just an hour, maybe an hour and a half."

"Take all the time you need. We'll be fine."

An hour later Evelyn walked back into the nursery to find Alice, Darren, Helen, Marisa, and Jeff gathered around the fountain display.

"What's this about? Another plot?" She looked at the front door to watch for Jamie's entrance.

"No," Jeff stepped forward to embrace her. "We're here to apologize. We just wanted to help. It looks like we just made it harder on you, though."

"That's right." Alice joined them in the embrace. "Rejection is hard enough once. It shouldn't happen again and again."

"It's okay." She stepped back and looked at the little group. "I guess they never got around to your turn, Helen."

She smiled uneasily. "It's a good thing. I was thinking of another party, but come to think of it, you were humiliated enough at the first one."

"That one wasn't your fault. It was my idea not to tell Jamie I was coming. So, I guess I'm just as guilty as you guys. I plotted, too."

"Well, we're sorry, Ev." Marisa stepped forward and hugged her.

"I got in on this late, Evelyn." Darren said. "I should have listened to Alice. She warned me not to get involved."

Alice took his hand. "My warning was a little weak, though. I have to admit I thought your idea was pretty good."

"We hope you'll forgive us," Jeff said.

"Oh, Dad." She hated the fact that her nose started to run. The tears in her eyes spilled out and ran down her cheek.

"Here." Jeff pulled a handkerchief out of his pocket.

Evelyn laughed and took it. "I can't believe you still carry one of these. It isn't used, is it?"

"No, I got a fresh one before I left the house, for you."

She looked up at him and couldn't stifle the sob that escaped.

"So, will you forgive us?" Alice asked.

She looked at the little group in front of her. "Forgive you for being such good friends and family that you cared enough to interfere? I think I should be grateful for that."

"We do care that much," Marisa said. "I'm going to give my brother a good talking to the next time I see him."

"Please don't. It won't help."

Marisa bowed her head.

Helen stepped forward and put her hand on Evelyn's shoulder. "We want you to forgive us for not being straightforward with you. I guess we were somewhat dishonest. And that was wrong."

"That's true, but not unexpected with Alice as the ring leader."

"Hey, how do you know it was me?

Evelyn and Jeff looked at her.

"Well, okay, it was me. So, what about it? Can you forgive us?"

She looked at them all standing there and dabbed at a fresh flow of tears. "You're forgiven and appreciated. Thanks for caring."

They all rushed to her and enjoyed a group hug.

"Honey," Jeff said. They all stepped back and dabbed at their eyes. "Why don't you go on home and get some rest. You look so tired. I hate to see you look so tired. I'll stay for the afternoon."

"Will Mom be okay?"

"She's doing great! She went for a jog this morning. I'm beginning to relax."

"Good," she smiled. "I think I'll go then."

*

Chapter 11

She worked on Sunday. She was usually off, but she was filling in for Darcy. Darcy would be back on Tuesday. Evelyn planned to try to work out a long weekend soon so she could get a little time away. Maybe she'd go down to the coast. Spend a few days at the beach.

Monday she felt better. The pain was still there. She was sure it would never go away, but it was becoming more bearable.

"So, I guess we're turning this place into a day care center again?" Darcy stood looking down at Bradley. Her hands were propped on her hips. She was scowling.

"This place never was a day care center, Darcy." Evelyn sighed. "Brad likes to come here. I don't mind helping Ruth out."

Bradley stood and put his hands on his hips in a remarkable imitation of Darcy. He scowled. "You know you don't mind having me here. I'm not a problem."

"I guess you're alright." She struggled not to laugh. "But don't come into my office and bother me like you did the last time. When I'm in there I have work to do. Speaking of which," she turned to Evelyn. "I have a little job I wonder if you would help me with."

"Of course, what is it."

"Come into the office. It's paperwork. I do think you need to see some of what goes on in the business side of the place."

"Yes, I agree. Let me finish up what I'm doing here I'll be right in." She turned to the display she'd been working on. Darcy went back to her office. Just as she was finishing up, the door opened and a waft of cool fall air swept in. She looked up and saw Jamie striding toward her.

"Jamie!" Bradley called and ran to greet him. He threw himself into Jamie's hands and was scooped off the ground and tossed in the air.

"Hey, kid. Hanging out at the nursery again?"

"Yeah, I like it a lot better here than with a babysitter. Can you imagine someone calling me a baby?"

Jamie set him back on the floor and looked down the considerable distance to where the child stood. "Imagine," he said.

"Hey, Ev." He looked in her direction. "I was just on my way up to see David. Good news. They've laid the foundation for the house and the Kennel. Next will be the cattery. They'll start work on the kennel next week. When that's finished they'll start work on the cattery. I can live in the shed for a little while longer."

He was beaming. "That's great, Jamie." She moved cautiously to where he stood and put her arms up for a hug. He leaned down and gave her a brief embrace then stepped back. His face was flaming.

"Ev," Bradley interrupted the awkward moment. "Jeff just walked past the window. See he's heading down the path toward the back greenhouse. I'm going to catch up with him. He might need some help in the greenhouse."

She looked out the window. Her dad was heading in that direction. "Okay, go ahead, but catch up with him and don't go off the path. Brad," she called. "Take your jacket. It's cold outside."

"Okay. Okay." He grabbed the jacket he had dropped onto a display shelf. "Remember I'm not a baby. I'm smarter than most grown-ups." He ran to the door, reached up to the knob and struggled to pull it open. Once it was open, he dashed through.

Jamie laughed. "The kid doesn't have a self-esteem problem, does he?"

"Not at all. It's good that he'll be with Dad for a while. I'm going to do some paperwork with Darcy. I don't think he'd like that very much."

"Will you like it?"

"I don't think so, but it's a part of the business I haven't done anything with. I need to know what's involved."

"Well, I'll go on up to see David. You go on into the office and have a good time." He laughed and headed toward the stairs to the café.

Evelyn watched him go then headed to the office.

Outside, Bradley watched as Jeff rounded the corner out of sight. He looked around. Finding nobody in the yard, he ran around the side of the building to Jamie's car. He tested the door handle. Good, it was unlocked. He wouldn't have to crawl through the plastic on the hatch back. He crawled over the seat, opened the lid to the trunk behind it and crawled in. He had to rearrange the tennis gear but finally he was relatively comfortable. He propped the top slightly open with his jacket for air and settled down to wait.

About an hour later Evelyn leaned back from the computer. She closed the spreadsheet she'd been working on and decided to go relieve her dad. He'd had the kid for long enough. Bradley's mom would be here in a while. She should make sure he wasn't too dirty to get into the car.

"Hey, Dad," she said as she walked up behind him. He was sitting at a potting table working on something. She put her arms around his neck and kissed his cheek. "I came to relieve you. Brad's mom will be here in a little while. I thought I'd better clean him up and see if he has any homework.

"What are you talking about?"

"Stop kidding, Dad. Where's he hiding?"

"Evelyn, I haven't seen him in hours."

The hair prickled on the back of her neck. "Please tell me you're kidding. You walked by the window and he wanted to go with you. You weren't that far ahead. There was plenty of time for him to catch up."

Jeff stood up and put his hand on her shoulder. "Calm down, honey. I'm sure there's an explanation."

"He's my responsibility. I should have known better than to let him go, but you were right there."

"Well, come on, let's look for him. I'm sure he just got distracted with something. He's probably designing a landscape, maybe even a fountain now that he's mastered his problem." Jeff laughed uneasily.

"Evelyn?" Darcy ran into the greenhouse. "Thank god I found you. Jamie just called my office. He said he's been trying to get you on your cell phone."

"I don't have it with me. I left it at home. I don't have time to talk to him now. Bradley is missing." Evelyn started to push past Darcy.

"No, he isn't." Darcy stopped her with a hand on her arm. "He's with Jamie. Apparently, he hid in the back of his car and took a ride out to the rescue. He wanted to see it."

"That little monster!" Evelyn sighed. "What a relief. I didn't know how I was going to tell Ruth I lost her son."

"Well," Darcy said. "Jamie needs someone to go out there to get the kid. You know there's only one seat belt in that car and Bradley can't drive." She laughed. "He probably could, but it isn't legal."

"I can't believe he didn't just dump that car last week when it looked dead" Evelyn ran her hand through her hair.

"Jamie tends to put himself last," Jeff said. "I'd go with you, honey," he kissed her cheek, "but your mom will be here any minute. We're going to the mall. She says if she can't look dumpy, I can't either." He smiled. "I hate to shop, but I wouldn't want to look dumpy."

"Wait a minute." Evelyn looked back and forth at the two of them. "This isn't another set up, is it?"

"Hey." Jeff put up his hands. "We've apologized. We've all learned our lesson."

"I don't do things like that, Evelyn." Darcy looked so serious Evelyn had to laugh.

"No, you don't."

"Do you want me to go out to get him? I will, but you'll have to stay until I get back."

"No thanks, Darcy. I appreciate it, but it's my responsibility. Well, I'd better go on. I'll call Ruth and tell her what happened. I'll take him home. I won't be back this afternoon."

"Okay, honey," Jeff said. "Don't be too mad at him."

"I won't. He's been asking me to take him out there. He and Jamie have become such good friends. Maybe if I'd done it this wouldn't have happened."

Forty-five minutes later Evelyn pulled down the gravel driveway to the shed. Jamie and Bradley sat at the picnic table drinking something out of plastic cups. She got out of the car and crossed her arms.

Jamie stood up. "I'm sorry, Ev. From now on I'm going to check that trunk before I go anywhere."

"It's not your fault, Jamie. It's Bradley's fault. You know, Bradley." She held up her hand as he started to object. "Don't tell me not to call you Bradley This may put a stop to you joining me at the nursery in the afternoons. Was it worth it?"

"Mom wouldn't do that. She knows the nursery is an educational place for me."

"Maybe she wouldn't do it but I might."

"Oh no." He jumped down from the bench and ran to her. "Please don't, Ev. I won't do anything like this again. I promise. I just wanted to see it so bad and you wouldn't take me."

There were tears in his eyes and he looked up at her imploringly. She felt herself softening and looked over at Jamie. He covered his smile with his hand. She stooped down to his level and opened her arms. He rushed into them and buried his face in her shoulder. He cried for just a minute then pulled gently away and wiped at his eyes with his fists.

"We'd better get back. Your mom was very understanding when I called her. However, I don't think we should keep her waiting too long."

"You already told her?"

"Yes, I did. So, let's get going."

"I need to use the facilities."

Jamie laughed. "... the facilities? You know where they are."

"It might take a little while." Bradley rocked back and forth on his heels.

"Are you alright?" Evelyn asked, concerned."

"I have to poop."

"Oh, okay." She looked at Jamie. He was looking at the sky. "Do you need any help?"

Bradley looked disgusted. "Come on, Ev, I know how to poop by myself." He turned and ran in the direction of the mobile homes.

"Well." She looked back at Jamie. "This might take a little while."

"Would you like a glass of wine or anything?"

"No, I can drive on one glass of wine, but I don't feel comfortable with the kid in the car."

"I see your point." Jamie shuffled his feet and turned his back to her. He looked into the forest for a minute then turned back. "Listen, Evelyn, I want to talk to you about something. Maybe we could arrange a time to sit down and talk."

He sounded so serious it worried her. He never called her Evelyn. "What is it, Jamie? Is something wrong?"

"Yes, there is something wrong."

"What?" She went to him and laid her hand on his arm. "Did something happen to the loan. Are you sick or something?"

He laughed. "Nothing happened to the loan. I'm okay, except that I'm an idiot."

"No, you're not!" She stepped back. "And if you're going to start that business about me being better off without you again, I'll put my hands over my ears. I won't listen."

"I'm pretty sure you would be better off without me ..."

She put her hands over her ears and started to hum.

Jamie took her wrists and pulled them away. "But I can't live without *you*."

She blinked and looked up at him.

"I tried. Don't say I didn't try. But I can't do it." He leaned down and brushed her lips with his. He smiled down at her. "Close your mouth, Ev. It's hard to kiss you with your mouth hanging open like that."

"Say that again, Jamie."

"Close your mouth ..."

"Not that. The other thing."

"I can't live without you. I was wrong to just try to break it off. I thought if I could stay away from you it wouldn't hurt so bad. I was wrong. See, I'm not so good. I guess I should have talked to you about it. I was afraid you'd talk me out of it. I should have let you."

"Jamie." She stepped up to him and put her arms around his neck. "I want you to stop talking and kiss me. This time I'll close my mouth.""

He lowered his mouth to hers. It was warm and sweet. The kiss was perfect, gentle at first then soon became more urgent.

"Well it's about time!"

They stepped apart to look at Bradley. He stood with his small arms crossed over his chest.

"So, Bradley," Evelyn said. "Was this little plot your idea or did my sister help you with it."

"She helped me inadvertently. I'm sure if she'd known why I was plying her with all those questions, she wouldn't have been so talkative. She gave me some ideas without knowing it."

"Well." Jamie put his arm around Evelyn's shoulders. "Thanks, Brad, your plot worked when all the others failed."

"It may have worked but it took long enough. I was starting to think *I* would have to propose to her to get you to pay attention."

They stepped apart at the sound of cars approaching on the gravel drive. Jeff's car came into view first. Amanda was in the passenger seat. Alice and Marisa were in the back. Ruth's car approached next. Adam was with her and Helen and Darcy sat in the back.

"So, the whole team is here." She called as they all filed out of the cars.

"We're not part of the team," Ruth said. She and Adam each took one of Bradley's hands and glared down at him.

Evelyn laughed. She couldn't feel mad at anyone or anything. "So, you were in on this after all, Darcy."

"Absolutely not!" Darcy stepped around the open car door and walked toward Jamie. "I don't plot. I've decided it's time for me to wring your stupid neck."

Jamie stepped back.

"It's time you stopped pretending you don't love this girl and fess up to it. Maybe you are a tennis coach. Maybe she is a successful business woman. So what? Both of those things are respectable things to do. So, knock it off! You're breaking her heart."

The whole group stood silent for a minute.

"Okay," Jamie said.

"And another thing ..." Darcy pointed her finger at him then stopped. "Okay?"

"He said okay, Darcy." Jeff stepped up beside her. "I guess your idea of the direct approach worked."

"In fact," Jamie said as he lowered to one knee. "Ouch!" He rolled to his side and grabbed his leg.

"What's wrong, Jamie?" Evelyn fell to her knees beside him. "Something's wrong with him, Mom. He fell."

"He didn't fall, honey." Amanda looked down at Jamie. His face was very red.

He shook his head and laughed. "I was going down on one knee but I put it on a rock." He rolled to a kneeling position. "I don't know if it's right for both of us to be on our knees, but Evelyn, will you marry me?"

"You want me to marry you? Oh, Jamie." She launched herself at him. "Yes, yes, yes!"

A loud cheer went up from the group. The trailer that housed the dogs vibrated with a chorus of howls.

"Wait here." Jamie stood, ducked into his hut and returned in seconds with a small velvet sack. He pulled Evelyn to her feet. "I couldn't afford a ring, but my dad gave me this." He pulled a ring out of the sack and held it out to her. "It was my Great Aunt Marge's engagement ring. Unfortunately, she had some kind of mental breakdown before her wedding so she never was able to wear it. I don't think it's bad luck or anything, though." He knew he was rambling. "My grandma gave it to Dad for Mom, but he'd already bought her one. So, he kept it and gave it to me. The diamond is only a half karat and the setting is really plain."

Evelyn took the ring from him and looked at it. It was beautiful. Small and simple, just the kind of thing she liked.

"It'll fit." Jamie went on. "I had it sized. Remember I got you that ring before you went away to school. I remember your ring size."

"It's beautiful, Jamie." She slipped it on her finger. She looked up, her eyes swimming with tears.

"Maybe later we could get you another one if you want ..."

"Jamie, don't talk anymore. Just kiss me."

www.ingramcontent.com/pod-product-compliance
Lightning Source LLC
LaVergne TN
LVHW041541070426
835507LV00011B/871